How to Conduct Self-Administered and Mail Surveys
2nd edition

THE SURVEY KIT, Second Edition

Purposes: The purposes of this 10-volume Kit are to enable readers to prepare and conduct surveys and to help readers become better users of survey results. Surveys are conducted to collect information; surveyors ask questions of people on the telephone, face-to-face, and by mail. The questions can be about attitudes, beliefs, and behavior as well as socioeconomic and health status. To do a good survey, one must know how to plan and budget for all survey tasks, how to ask questions, how to design the survey (research) project, how to sample respondents, how to collect reliable and valid information, and how to analyze and report the results.

Users: The Kit is for students in undergraduate and graduate classes in the social and health sciences and for individuals in the public and private sectors who are responsible for conducting and using surveys. Its primary goal is to enable users to prepare surveys and collect data that are accurate and useful for primarily practical purposes. Sometimes, these practical purposes overlap with the objectives of scientific research, and so survey researchers will also find the Kit useful.

Format of the Kit: All books in the series contain instructional objectives, exercises and answers, examples of surveys in use and illustrations of survey questions, guidelines for action, checklists of dos and don'ts, and annotated references.

Volumes in The Survey Kit:

1. **The Survey Handbook, 2nd**
   Arlene Fink
2. **How to Ask Survey Questions, 2nd**
   Arlene Fink
3. **How to Conduct Self-Administered and Mail Surveys, 2nd**
   Linda B. Bourque and Eve P. Fielder
4. **How to Conduct Telephone Surveys, 2nd**
   Linda B. Bourque and Eve P. Fielder
5. **How to Conduct In-Person Interviews for Surveys, 2nd**
   Sabine Mertens Oishi
6. **How to Design Survey Studies, 2nd**
   Arlene Fink
7. **How to Sample in Surveys, 2nd**
   Arlene Fink
8. **How to Assess and Interpret Survey Psychometrics, 2nd**
   Mark S. Litwin
9. **How to Manage, Analyze, and Interpret Survey Data, 2nd**
   Arlene Fink
10. **How to Report on Surveys, 2nd**
    Arlene Fink

Linda B. Bourque & Eve P. Fielder

How to Conduct Self-Administered and Mail Surveys

2nd edition

THE SURVEY KIT

SAGE Publications
International Educational and Professional Publisher
Thousand Oaks ■ London ■ New Delhi

For information:

Sage Publications, Inc.
2455 Teller Road
Thousand Oaks, California 91320
E-mail: order@sagepub.com

Sage Publications Ltd.
6 Bonhill Street
London EC2A 4PU
United Kingdom

Sage Publications India Pvt. Ltd.
M-32 Market
Greater Kailash I
New Delhi 110 048 India

Printed in the United States of America

Library of Congress Cataloging-in-Publication Data

The survey kit.—2nd ed.
        p. cm.
Includes bibliographical references.
ISBN 0-7619-2510-4 (set : pbk.)
1. Social surveys. 2. Health surveys. I. Fink, Arlene.
HN29 .S724 2002
300'.723—dc21   2002012405

This book is printed on acid-free paper.

02 03 04 05 10 9 8 7 6 5 4 3 2 1

Acquisitions Editor:	C. Deborah Laughton
Editorial Assistant:	Veronica Novak
Copy Editor:	Judy Selhorst
Production Editor:	Diane S. Foster
Typesetter:	Bramble Books
Proofreader:	Cheryl Rivard
Cover Designer:	Ravi Balasuriya
Production Designer:	Michelle Lee

Contents

Acknowledgments

We would like to thank Arlene Fink for her invitation to participate in this series and her helpful comments on earlier drafts of this manuscript; Tonya Hays, Terry Silberman, and Elizabeth Stephenson for their assistance in finding materials used in the examples; Marilyn Hart and Christopher Corey for technical assistance; and Gloria Krauss for clerical and editing assistance. We particularly want to thank Deborah Riopelle, project coordinator for the Workplace Assault Study, for her assistance in putting together examples from that study; and Maggie Robbins of the Service Employees International Union (SEIU), Bart Deiner of SEIU Local 660, and Wilma Cadorna of SEIU Local 535, who expedited the development and administration of the Workplace Assault Study. Scott Perez, David Watson, Kerry Sheffer, and other staff from the Southern California Injury Prevention Research Center (SCIPRC) provided clerical assistance for the second edition, and Jess F. Kraus, director of SCIPRC, provided us with space where we could hide from our other obligations during the period of revision.

The respondent letter used for the college student survey came from a study conducted by Jim Sidanius and Marilynn Brewer, funded by the Russell Sage Foundation (Attitudes About Cultural Diversity Among a College Population, Grant No. RSF 879.301). Data used in examples from the Prospective Evaluation for Radial Keratotomy (PERK) Study were collected and processed with funds from the National Eye Institute (Grant Nos. EY03752 and EY03761); data used in examples from the Workplace Assault Study were collected and processed with funds from the Southern California Injury Prevention Research Center under Grant No. R49-CCR903622 from the Centers for Disease Control.

How to Conduct Self-Administered and Mail Surveys: Learning Objectives

The aim of this book is to demonstrate how to develop and administer self-administered surveys, including online or Internet-based surveys and with particular attention to mail surveys. Areas covered include the kinds of self-administered questionnaires, the circumstances under which they are appropriately used, and the skills you need to design them, estimate the cost of self-administered surveys, select appropriate samples, and document the decisions made.

The specific objectives are as follows:

- Describe the types of self-administered questionnaires

- Identify the advantages and disadvantages of the use of self-administered questionnaires

- Identify the advantages and disadvantages of the use of Internet-based questionnaires

- Decide whether a self-administered questionnaire is appropriate for your survey question

- Determine the content of the questionnaire

- Develop questions for a user-friendly questionnaire

- Pretest, pilot-test, and revise questions

- Format a user-friendly questionnaire

- Write advance letters and cover letters that motivate and increase response rates

- Write specifications that describe the reasons for and sources of the questions on the questionnaire and the methodology used in administering the study

- Describe how to develop and produce a sample, identify potential resources for a sample, organize the sample, determine sample size, and increase response rates

- Inventory materials and procedures involved in mail and self-administered surveys

- Describe follow-up procedures for nonrespondents, methods of tracking respondents, and number and timing of follow-up attempts

- Describe how returned questionnaires are processed, edited, and coded

- Describe data entry

- Describe how records are kept

- Estimate the costs of a self-administered or mail survey

- Estimate personnel needs for a self-administered or mail survey

- Fully document the development and administration of the questionnaire and the data collected with it

1 Overview of Self-Administered Questionnaires

Self-administered **questionnaires** are one of the most frequently used methods for collecting data in research studies. Furthermore, self-administered questionnaires appear in many areas of our lives. Think, for example, of the testing strategies used in most classrooms, from kindergarten through graduate school. A classroom test is a type of self-administered questionnaire. Similarly, we fill out forms—also types of questionnaires—to obtain everything from driver's licenses to death certificates.

Unfortunately, this very proliferation and familiarity of self-administered questionnaires in a wide variety of daily life settings results in assumptions on the part of many neophyte surveyors that they can develop self-administered questionnaires literally overnight and use them to collect data that will be available immediately. Like any research endeavor and the use of any procedure for collecting data, the development and implementation of a **survey** using self-administered questionnaires take time and thought. This book outlines the circumstances under which self-administered questionnaires are a good or at least adequate method for collecting information, what surveyors must consider in designing such questionnaires, and the methods surveyors can use to induce respondents to complete such question-naires while maximizing the collection of complete, reliable, and valid data.

Types of Self-Administered Questionnaires

Self-administered questionnaires are instruments used to collect information from people who complete the instru-ments themselves. The stimulus in such questionnaires is exclusively visual. As we have noted, such instruments are not used exclusively for research purposes; they can be used to collect information for a wide variety of purposes and in a wide variety of settings. Until recent years, self-administered questionnaires have almost always been administered using **paper-and-pencil techniques**, but with the rapid prolifera-tion of personal computers and the growth of the informa-tion superhighway, the procedures associated with these questionnaires are increasingly being adapted to electronic media. To the extent that such developments are occurring, it is entirely possible that self-administered questionnaires disseminated online could add auditory stimuli to the visual in soliciting information, in much the same way that sophis-ticated voice-mail systems now route telephone requests for information, service, or appointments. For the purposes of this book, however, we focus on the traditional method by which surveys using self-administered questionnaires have historically been carried out—namely, each respondent receives a printed questionnaire, which he or she fills out using a pen or pencil. We do discuss e-mail surveys and **online surveys** where appropriate, however. Generally, we focus on online surveys in those instances, because they are considered the more desirable approach to electronic **data collection**.

There are two types of self-administered questionnaires, best described as the ends of a unidimensional continuum. At one end are questionnaires that people answer in the presence of the surveyor or other supervisory personnel. At the opposite end of the continuum are questionnaires completed by respondents outside the presence of the surveyor or other monitoring personnel.

Questionnaires sent through the mail provide the most common example of unsupervised administration. Such questionnaires—frequently called **mail questionnaires**—are the major focus of this book, both because of their frequent use and because almost everything that applies to a mail questionnaire has equal applicability to self-administered questionnaires distributed through other means and administered in other environments (such as e-mail and online surveys). Before we turn our attention to mail questionnaires, we briefly describe below some of the different kinds of supervised or partially supervised environments in which self-administered questionnaires are distributed.

SUPERVISED ADMINISTRATION

One-to-One Supervision

In the most extreme form of supervised administration, the respondent is in a one-to-one situation with the surveyor and the surveyor is available to answer any questions that the respondent has about the questionnaire. This type of **administration** is rarely used because it is very expensive, and, as we discuss later, a major reason surveyors choose to use self-administered questionnaires is to reduce costs. The costs associated with one-to-one supervision of respondents completing self-administered questionnaires more closely resemble those of telephone or in-person interviewing than those of self-administration.

Nonetheless, surveyors do use one-to-one supervision on occasion—often within the context of studies in which **in-person (or face-to-face)** interviewing is the major method of data collection. For example, under the auspices of the

National Institute for Drug Abuse, a self-administered questionnaire was developed for use in ascertaining respondents'
current and historical use of drugs. The questionnaire was
given to each respondent as part of an in-person interview.
The format of the questionnaire was such that the time
taken to complete it did not differ depending on the respondent's current or past drug history. In other words, a person
who had never used drugs took just as long to complete the
questionnaire as did someone who had used many drugs.
Within the context of the in-person interview, elaborate procedures were developed to ensure that the interviewer did
not see the self-administered questionnaire, either while it
was being completed or once it was completed. The purpose
of these precautions was to maximize **confidentiality**, the
assumption being that people generally underreport their
use of drugs. At the same time, the interviewer was available
to answer questions or to clarify concepts if necessary.

Group Administration

Far more common than one-to-one supervision are situations in which questionnaires are passed out in classrooms,
workplaces, or other group settings. In such **group administration**, each person is expected to complete the questionnaire without consulting other persons in the group, but the
surveyor or another supervisory person is available to provide introductory instructions, answer questions, and monitor the extent to which questionnaires are completed and
individual respondents communicate with each other during the period of administration. Depending on the purpose
of the study, this administrator may be instructed to answer
and clarify any and all questions that come up or may be
instructed to defer or deflect all or most questions.

For example, when group self-administration is being
used to develop a questionnaire, the surveyor will probably
want to learn as much as possible about how the questionnaire "works," whether respondents understand the questions asked, whether the information requested is accessible
to respondents, and whether the response categories pro-

vided are exhaustive, mutually exclusive, and readily understood. In such instances, the surveyor may invite respondents to raise questions as they move through the questionnaire, or, alternatively, the surveyor may ask the respondents to complete the questionnaire first and then solicit questions and comments as part of a general discussion afterward. In either case, the person supervising the group administration must keep careful notes of the issues raised by respondents, because many of their questions and comments may reveal problems that will necessitate changes in the questionnaire.

In contrast, when a finalized questionnaire is being administered in a group setting, supervisory personnel often are instructed to deflect any questions or comments raised by respondents. Many of the instruments that survey researchers currently use to measure attitudes, opinions, physical health status, psychological distress, and a number of other things were developed to be administered as paper-and-pencil tests in either individual or group settings. Generally, these instruments have been developed over time, and substantial attention has been paid to the establishment of their validity and reliability. They also have been developed to assess how particular individual respondents compare with other groups of respondents. When such instruments are administered, the surveyor wants to do everything possible to ensure that all respondents receive an identical stimulus and that the information obtained from each represents that individual's feelings, attitudes, or health status. In such cases, the administrator in a group setting will generally use a scripted set of instructions to introduce the questionnaire. These instructions may or may not be repeated on the questionnaire itself. Included in the instructions will be a statement to the effect that there are no right or wrong answers to the questions being asked; rather, the purpose is to find out how this particular person feels about or experiences the topic under investigation. When pertinent, instructions are also given on how to complete the questionnaire.

Semisupervised Administration

In group administrations, as described above, it is assumed for our purposes that everyone is in the same place—usually a room—for the duration of the administration period or at least for the beginning part of it. Everyone hears the same set of verbal instructions, and everyone's questions or comments are handled in similar ways. Self-administered questionnaires are also completed in an almost infinite variety of situations where **semisupervised administration** is the norm. For example, the receptionist in the waiting room of a well-baby clinic might distribute questionnaires. In such a situation, the receptionist gives no formal presentation of verbal instructions to the potential group of respondents as a whole; rather, each respondent receives pertinent instructions when he or she is given the questionnaire. Because personnel may change during the week and the activity level in the clinic may vary, the content and extent of instructions that different respondents receive are also likely to vary. Respondents who arrive when the clinic is quiet may receive detailed instructions, whereas those who arrive when the patient load is heavy may receive no instructions. Clearly, the consistency of the stimulus provided in such situations, at least as indicated in instructions, has the potential to influence the validity and reliability of the data obtained. Nonetheless, someone—in this case the receptionist—is, at least titularly, available to answer questions about the questionnaire and monitor the data collection effort at some minimal level.

Questionnaires are also passed out in environments such as registration lines, auditoriums, amusement centers, and airplanes, and as persons are entering or exiting stores and other sites. The administration of such questionnaires can also be considered semisupervised to the extent that the person who distributes and collects the questionnaires is available to answer questions and provide instructions. The amount of control the surveyor exerts in such an environment is, however, limited to the selection of who will receive a questionnaire, the ability to ensure that distributed questionnaires are completed and returned, and the consistency with which any verbal instructions beyond those printed on the hard copy of the questionnaire are, in fact, solicited by or available to respondents.

UNSUPERVISED ADMINISTRATION

To our knowledge, no statistics are available regarding the number of self-administered questionnaires that are used in research projects or how they distribute between supervised and **unsupervised administration,** but when people think of self-administered questionnaires within a research context, in all probability they are thinking of questionnaires sent through the mail, which is still the primary method of distributing unsupervised self-administered questionnaires. Online self-administered surveys are gaining in usage, however, especially in areas such as internal employee studies, organizational surveys, and household panel studies.

When questionnaire administration is completely unsupervised, it is imperative that the questionnaire be completely self-sufficient, or able to stand alone. When questionnaires are sent through the mail, no member of the research staff is available to answer respondents' questions or to ensure that the correct persons (or, indeed, anyone) complete the questionnaires. Even though the cover sheet that accompanies a mailed questionnaire might include a contact name and phone number for the potential respondent's use if he or she needs clarification or information, the respondent must initiate such contact, and so must be highly motivated to seek information.

The remainder of this book focuses on the design of mail questionnaires, because the requirement that they be able to stand alone places great restrictions on what surveyors can include in them and requires surveyors to pay careful attention to how clearly the questions are written and presented so as to maximize response rates.

Example 1.1 presents a summary of the advantages and disadvantages of using the four different ways of administering questionnaires discussed above.

EXAMPLE 1.1
Four Ways of Administering
Respondent-Completed Questionnaires

Type of Administration	Advantages	Disadvantages
One-to-one	Interviewer available to answer questions	Expensive
	Maximizes confidentiality in face-to-face interviews	
	Provides in-depth data on the answerability of questions	
Group	Allows for consistency in instructions to respondents	Not usable with general populations
	Simultaneous administration to all respondents	
	Administrator can answer questions	
	Provides some information on the answerability of questions	
	Allows administrator to monitor communication between respondents	
	Allows administrator to monitor completion by respondents	
	Useful in pretesting	

Example 1.1 continued

Type of Administration	Advantages	Disadvantages
Semisupervised	Administrator can answer questions Efficient Allows administrator some ability to monitor communication between respondent and others Allows administrator some ability to monitor completion Useful in pretesting Inexpensive	Samples are frequently unrepresentative Instructions may be inconsistent
Unsupervised	Allows for consistent stimulus to all respondents Allows for the possibility of more representative samples	Lack of control over who responds Provides no direct information on the answerability of questions Questionnaire must stand alone

Advantages of Self-Administered Questionnaires

COST

The single greatest advantage of self-administered questionnaires is their lower cost compared with other methods (e.g., in-person and telephone interviews). Given questionnaires of the same length and the same survey objective, a completed questionnaire administered by mail costs approximately 50% less than one administered by telephone and 75% less than one administered by in-person interview.

SAMPLING

Mail surveys have three sample-related advantages over other kinds of surveys: They allow for wider geographic coverage, larger samples, and wider coverage within a sample population. Although these three sampling issues are interrelated with one another as well as with issues of cost, we discuss each advantage briefly below.

Geographic Coverage

Mail (and online) surveys allow for wide geographic coverage, especially in comparison with surveys that use in-person interviewing. A questionnaire can be mailed (or made available through the Internet) anywhere in the world, whereas in-person interviews tend to be restricted to defined geographic areas or areas where trained **interviewers** are available, can be monitored, and are able to contact intended respondents physically. **Telephone interviewing** also allows for wider geographic coverage than in-person interviewing, and, for all practical intents and purposes, can be conducted anywhere within the United States from a single site, assuming that funds are available to cover long-distance charges and the population under study has access to telephones. Telephone interviewing becomes problematic, however, if a substantial number of the designated respondents reside outside the United States.

In one survey, for example, we used mail questionnaires to contact both undergraduate and graduate alumni of UCLA. Although most of the potential respondents lived in the United States (many of them in Southern California), a proportion of both groups resided in other countries. Because little money was available for the study, data collection using either telephone or in-person interviewing techniques would have prevented us from attempting to obtain information from non-U.S. residents. In contrast, sending questionnaires through the mail allowed us to contact a substantial proportion of such respondents and yielded response rates comparable to those of the sample as a whole. Online surveys may be ideal for future studies of similar populations—that is, populations made up of individuals who are likely to have Internet access, who are found in preexisting sample lists, and who can receive e-mail notices asking them to visit a Web site and fill out a questionnaire.

Larger Samples

The lower unit cost of a mail questionnaire combined with the mail survey's ability to cover a wide geographic area with little additional cost for respondents at a distance allows surveyors to study a larger sample of persons or groups. Thus, where available funds might allow for an interview survey to contact only 100 persons within a limited geographic area, the same amount of money may allow a surveyor to mail questionnaires to 400-500 persons over a much larger geographic area. As access to the Internet becomes more widespread, large online sample surveys over wide geographic areas will become more feasible.

Wider Coverage Within a Sample Population

Some people are reluctant to talk with anyone they do not know, either in person or on the phone. This reluctance to talk with strangers has increased in recent years, particularly in large urban areas. For example, it may be difficult or impossible for a surveyor to convince residents of a high-security building to agree to be interviewed—particularly if the interviews are to be conducted in the respondents' homes. These same persons may, however, be willing to respond to a mail or online questionnaire. Similarly, some persons who do not have access to telephones or are reluctant to be interviewed by telephone may be willing and able to respond to a self-administered questionnaire.

In some cases, respondents who do not want to make a commitment to an interviewer to be available at an appointed time for a specific length of time to do an interview may be more than willing to complete a self-administered questionnaire, because they can do it at their convenience.

IMPLEMENTATION

Surveys using mail and other self-administered questionnaires are much easier to implement than other kinds of surveys. First, the number of personnel needed is substantially lower, because there is no need for interviewers and those who hire, train, and supervise them. As we discuss in Chapter 2, self-administered questionnaires are shorter and simpler in structure than the kinds of questionnaires used in interview surveys, so once the data are obtained, fewer personnel and less complicated procedures are required to process them. In contrast to telephone interviewing, and particularly **computer-assisted telephone interviewing (CATI)**, minimal equipment is needed to conduct a survey by mail. In the simplest case, a single person can conduct an entire mail survey from start to finish.

The implementation of online surveys has some of the same challenges posed by CATI: The surveyor needs appropriate computer equipment and survey software, plus a programmer or technician skilled in the application of this software, to conduct an online survey. Surveyors should not attempt to launch their own online surveys until they have gained some experience in both survey research and Internet operations. Those with little expertise in these areas would be wiser to employ organizations or individuals with experience in the development and conduct of online surveys to handle the programming and administration.

When conducted by experts using the right materials, however, online surveys have the advantage of providing relatively clean data that require little or no end-stage processing. Commercially available software for online surveys can eliminate the possibility of missing data (by preventing respondents from skipping questions), allow for branching, prevent the entry of nonallowable codes, rotate question and/or response category order, and compile responses as they are collected. Some of the latest technology associated with online survey software can include pictorial stimuli or illustrations to accompany text. It should be noted that this option is relatively new, and surveyors who use it should allow time for adequate testing of their questionnaires to be sure that the images they select for use represent the associated content equally well across all population subgroups.

An individual or organization that wants to conduct an online survey but has little or no technological capability can contract with one of the numerous commercial vendors that conduct such surveys. The client can either provide or purchase the sample as appropriate, and also provide the survey instrument. The vendor has the computer hardware and software, the Internet site, and the technical expertise. Typically, the vendor can provide the client with a final product in any form from raw data to a written report summarizing the survey findings.

TIMING

Unlike almost all other methods of data collection, it can be assumed that when a questionnaire is sent through the mail, all members of the sample receive it nearly simultaneously. Thus the potential influence on respondents' experiences, opinions, or attitudes that might come from events outside of or unrelated to the study is reduced and can be assumed to be equal for all recipients of the questionnaire. For example, in a study we conducted concerning assault in the workplace, all questionnaires were mailed on the same day and were received by all respondents within the same 2- or 3-day period. Imagine conducting telephone interviews with the same group of respondents. In a methodologically rigorous telephone survey, it is generally not possible to conduct 1,000 interviews within a 2- or 3-day period—more likely, it would take weeks or even months. Suppose that during that period of time, an employee of the Los Angeles County Health Department is assaulted on the job and this assault is prominently featured in the *Los Angeles Times*. Clearly, persons interviewed *after* that assault are likely to have different attitudes and opinions about assault in the workplace than those interviewed *before* the assault. The two groups of respondents (those interviewed before the publicized assault and those interviewed after) cannot be assumed to have had their responses influenced identically by outside events. In contrast, had all respondent groups received questionnaires on the same day, they could be assumed to have been exposed to a similar stimulus. This is not to say that an event cannot occur at some point during the conduct of a mailed survey that might influence some respondents but not others; however, the "window of opportunity" for such an event is greatly lessened.

SENSITIVE TOPICS

Earlier, we discussed the use of self-administered questionnaires to collect information about drug use within the context of an interview. Many surveyors believe that people are more likely to give complete and truthful information on such **sensitive topics** in a self-administered questionnaire than in an interview. Early methodological studies tended to support this perception, but more recent studies suggest that surveyors may collect sensitive information as effectively or with even greater accuracy through telephone and in-person interviews. The variation in findings on this topic across time and studies can probably be accounted for by the overall objectives of the survey studies examined, the environments in which they were conducted, the ability of the interviewers in the studies to establish rapport, the extent to which respondents believed that the data they provided would be both anonymous and confidential, and the ways in which both the overall questionnaires and individual questions were structured. We are of the opinion that surveyors can effectively study sensitive topics using all kinds of questionnaires.

Online surveys and surveys conducted via e-mail pose other issues of sensitivity and confidentiality. Responses sent by e-mail obviously are not anonymous, and although online surveys may be confidential, many people question the security of information exchanged on the Internet. Although we are unaware of any cases in which individuals have broken through the security measures put in place for any online survey, this is something surveyors should watch out for as the use of this survey technique becomes more widespread.

Disadvantages of Self-Administered Questionnaires

Mail and other self-administered questionnaires have a number of disadvantages that limit or prohibit their use in many research projects. These disadvantages can be grouped under three general headings: those related to sampling, those related to questionnaire construction, and those related to administration.

SAMPLING

Availability of Lists

Unfortunately, many neophyte researchers think that if a lot of people respond to their questionnaire, they have a "representative" **sample** that does not systematically exclude anyone and that their findings can therefore be generalized to people who are not included among the respondents. This is not the case; only **probability samples,** for which the characteristics of the larger **population** are known and the relationship of the sample to the population is known, are representative.

Although many surveys using self-administered questionnaires are conducted with admittedly nonrepresentative convenience samples, many surveyors want to use self-administered questionnaires, particularly mail question-naires, to collect data from samples that can be considered representative of the populations from which they are drawn. In order to do this—particularly when questionnaires are sent through the mail—a surveyor must have a complete and accurate list of the population of interest. To the extent that such a list is unavailable, incomplete, or inaccurate, the data obtained cannot be assumed to represent the popula-tion to which the surveyor wishes to generalize. In the worst-case scenario, the surveyor must either resort to other methods of sample generation and data collection (e.g., random-digit dialing and telephone interviewing), conduct a census to establish the population from which the sample is to be drawn, or resort to convenience sampling techniques.

Online surveys present a similar problem: Unless the sample is composed of the target universe and access to par-ticipation is tightly controlled, the results are likely to be nonrepresentative. An additional problem with online sur-veys is that of accessibility to the questionnaire: If access to the site is not controlled or restricted to a given range of identification markers, any individual who learns of or hap-pens across the site can complete the survey. Online surveys also present a new population coverage issue for researchers, as in recent years a new concept of social division has been introduced into American culture: the "digital divide." Simply put, most users of the Internet (and therefore most respondents for online surveys) are younger, more affluent, and more highly educated than the population at large.

Response Rates

One of the greatest and most studied disadvantages of using mail questionnaires is their low **response rate**. When a single mailing that incorporates no incentives is made to a sample of the general community, the surveyor can probably expect no better than a 20% response rate. The combined use of advance letters, follow-up contacts, incentives, and a variety of other procedures can increase response rates, but even in the best case, response rates for mail questionnaires are lower than those for telephone and in-person interviews.

To date, online survey response rates appear to fall well below those of mail surveys. Although response rates vary widely with the nature of the sample population, online surveys do not appear to be the answer to the ever-increasing dilemma of declining survey response rates. In a brief investigation of response rates across various online survey approaches, we found lows of around 5% to highs around 70%. Higher ranges were accomplished in professional membership organizations, where respondents would be expected to be highly motivated to participate. Although our investigation was by no means exhaustive, we believe that currently response rates in the range of 10% to 20% are common for online surveys. The recruitment strategies used in the various studies we looked at included e-mail invitations to organizational members; opt-in panels where e-mail addresses were obtained from a third party, such as a survey sample provider, or private consumer panels; pop-up surveys that appear on-screen when an individual is connected to an Internet site; and banner-advertised surveys that flash an invitation to visit the survey site while an individual is connected to a particular Internet site.

Whereas procedures exist for contacting nonresponders when questionnaires are delivered by mail, analogous procedures for contacting nonresponders in online surveys have not yet been developed—or at least they have not yet been reported in the literature.

Literacy and Language

One of the reasons response rates are poor—particularly in studies targeted at general community samples—is that persons who are illiterate or who have difficulty reading simply are unable to respond even if they want to. In the past, the rate of adult **illiteracy** in the United States was estimated to be 20%. Data from the 2000 U.S. Census show that 17.6% of the population over 5 years of age do not speak English in the home, that 44% of this group speaks English less than "very well," and that 6.9% of the population over age 25 has completed less than 9 years of schooling. Obviously, persons who are functionally illiterate are unable to complete a self-administered questionnaire and will be missed by *any* study in which they are part of the target population.

The visual acuity of potential respondents can also have an effect on response rates. Individuals who have problems with reading because they are visually impaired (such as the elderly) or dyslexic may find the effort required to read a questionnaire too great and may not complete and return it to the surveyor. Obviously, if visually impaired or dyslexic persons are overrepresented in the target population, the surveyor might be wise to consider an alternative method for collecting the data.

An additional problem—particularly in large urban areas on the East and West Coasts—is the wide range of languages spoken in American homes. For example, in Los Angeles County, 13% of the population is linguistically isolated (meaning that they speak no English), and an additional 26% report that a language other than English is the primary or only language spoken in the home, with 47.8% of this group speaking English less than "very well." Obviously, when a survey's target population includes a substantial proportion of potential respondents who are non-English speakers, the surveyor must arrange for **translation** of the questionnaire and must devise some mechanism for ensuring that each respondent receives a questionnaire in the correct language. As a result, it is generally not possible for surveyors to collect adequate or accurate data from multiple-language populations using self-administered questionnaires.

Online surveys face the same problems of **literacy** and language issues as do mail surveys. Although it is possible for an online survey to have multiple language versions of the questionnaire available on the survey Web site, many languages require the use of specialized character fonts on both the sending and receiving portals, and this can increase the complexity and cost of a given survey. Additionally, online survey respondents must be "computer literate" (e.g., they must be adept at using a mouse to click on appropriate responses) and must have access to computers that have the capability of accessing and downloading the questionnaire.

QUESTIONNAIRE CONSTRUCTION

Objective

A survey can be conducted using self-administered questionnaires only when the objective of the study is clear and not complex. For example, you would not want to use a mail questionnaire if you need to collect an entire occupational history on each respondent and you want to investigate each respondent's satisfaction with his or her current work site, job, employment benefits, and coworkers, and how these factors correlate with or interact with the respondent's lifestyle.

Obviously, surveyors hope to have motivated respondents in any research study, but **motivation** is particularly important when self-administered questionnaires are used for data collection. In the case of the study on workplace assault mentioned earlier, we decided that we could use mail questionnaires because union representatives informed us that many of their members had expressed concern about the physical safety of the environments where they worked. Thus we believed that potential respondents would consider the topic under study to be important, and that this heightened salience of the topic would increase respondents' motivation to participate in the study and hence increase our response rate.

Format

The need for a clear and noncomplex data collection objective has ramifications for how the questionnaire is constructed and precludes the use of many strategies typically used in questionnaire design. We discuss this issue in detail in Chapters 2 through 4, so we note only some of the limitations briefly here.

First, self-administered questionnaires must be shorter than questionnaires administered in other ways. If the questionnaire must be shorter, then obviously the number of questions asked and the number of topics covered are reduced. The importance of questionnaire length in online surveys, and its influence on response rates, has not been systematically studied. Researchers have experimented with including different kinds of **progress indicators** in online questionnaires to tell respondents what proportion they have completed and what proportion remains to completed. It is unknown at this time whether such progress indicators have any effect on response rates, or whether certain kinds of progress indicators are more effective than others.

Second, most of a self-administered questionnaire must be made up of **closed-ended questions.** Although highly motivated respondents may be willing to answer a few **open-ended questions,** the surveyor who writes a self-administered questionnaire dominated by such questions will find that few questionnaires will be returned, and those that are returned will frequently have substantial amounts of missing or irrelevant data. Online surveys face similar constraints: Most people do not like to write or type a lot of lengthy responses to open-ended questions.

Third, the self-administered questionnaire must stand alone. In other words, all the information the potential respondent needs to answer the questions must be provided on the questionnaire itself, as there is no interviewer available to clarify instructions or provide additional information to eliminate confusion. The surveyor's objective should be to make the questionnaire as easy as possible for the respondent to complete without assistance from others. This restriction means that cue cards or other visual aids cannot be used with self-administered questionnaires. It also means that the possible responses to each question must be limited to a number that respondents can readily assimilate and from which they can reasonably select those that apply to them. Thus the surveyor may not be able to include lists of mutually exclusive responses if such lists becomes excessively long. Nor should the surveyor expect respondents to be able to rank order large numbers of alternatives. Not only are such lists burdensome for respondents to read, assimilate, and select from, but they raise the issue of **primacy effect**— that is, respondents' tendency to select the *first* response they come to that reflects how they feel or behave even if it is not the best or most representative response available. Once respondents have selected their answers, they ignore the rest of the list and go to the next question. The necessity that the questionnaire be totally self-explanatory is probably one of the most difficult objectives for surveyors to achieve in the design of self-administered questionnaires.

Fourth, as part of the objective of simplifying the respondent's task, the surveyor needs to create a questionnaire without branches or skips. In other words, every question in the questionnaire should contain a response category that every respondent can comfortably use to describe his or her attitudes, behavior, knowledge, or characteristics. In some instances, this means that the surveyor should include a "not applicable" alternative among the responses provided for a question or series of questions. Some of the more technically complex (and, consequently, more costly) software for online surveys allows for **branching** and **skips,** but as complexity increases, the amount of time respondents must spend downloading questionnaires and responding to them also increases, with the result that such surveys are sometimes inaccessible to persons who do not have state-of-the-art computers.

Order Effects

When a questionnaire is administered by an in-person or telephone interviewer, the interviewer controls the order in which the questions are asked and controls whether or not the answer alternatives are made available to the respondent, either by reading aloud the alternatives or by presenting them in written form on a cue card. In a self-administered paper questionnaire, everything is simultaneously available to the respondent. (This is typically not true of online surveys, which usually do not allow a new screen of questions to appear until the respondent has completed the preceding screen.) With paper questionnaires, respondents can complete sections in any order they choose, and they can refer to one section while providing answers in another. Furthermore, a respondent can take a series of days or even weeks to complete a paper questionnaire. (The ability to self-administer portions of an online questionnaire over several sessions depends on the sophistication of the software. Some designs allow the respondent to reenter the questionnaire at a previous quit point at a later time, but some do not—in the latter case, if the respondent quits, this creates an "abandonment" or incomplete interview.)

Thus surveyors cannot use self-administered questionnaires when **order effect** might be an issue—that is, when one set of questions is likely to contaminate, bias, or influence respondents' answers to another section of the questionnaire. For example, political scientists and politicians often are interested in knowing what people perceive to be the greatest problems facing their communities. In an interview survey aimed at gathering such information, the questionnaire typically asks a series of questions designed to ascertain respondents' levels of concern over specific problems the surveyor assumes are faced by that community. When respondents have the ability to look ahead in the questionnaire and see the topics the surveyor has selected as problems for their community, they are more likely to mention the topics specifically asked about later in the questionnaire.

Similarly, it is not possible to build validity checks into survey studies that use paper self-administered questionnaires. If, for example, the surveyor is suspicious that respondents are more likely to underreport their age when asked, "How old were you on your last birthday?" than when they are asked, "When were you born?" a self-administered questionnaire would not be a good way to check the "match" between the answers given to the two questions, because respondents can compare their answers and change them to be consistent, if necessary. Opportunities for respondents to change their answers are significantly reduced or even eliminated when interviewers control the order in which questions are asked and have been given instructions regarding how they should proceed when respondents want to change any of their previous answers. The investigator may be able to build **validity** checks into a questionnaire for an online survey; this again depends on the sophistication of the software used.

ADMINISTRATION

Lack of Control Over Who Responds

The single biggest administrative disadvantage of using self-administered questionnaires is the fact that once the questionnaire leaves the surveyor's office, he or she has no **control** over who, in fact, fills it out and whether that person "consults" with others when completing it. For example, in the study on workplace assault mentioned previously, we had a list of the names and addresses of union members that was provided by the union. We addressed each cover letter and envelope to one union person. Once we sent the questionnaires out, however, we had no way to be sure that the designated respondent, who was a member of the union, completed the questionnaire, or, furthermore, that the designated respondent completed it without talking about it with other members of his or her household, workplace, or social group. Similar problems exist in online surveys. Unless the programming includes controls that prohibit a person from completing the questionnaire more than once, a respondent can reenter the Web site and complete the questionnaire multiple times. When controls or identifiers are added to self-administered questionnaires, respondents can be promised confidentiality, but they cannot be promised anonymity.

We know of a study conducted many years ago in which questionnaires were passed out by a receptionist in a clinic waiting room. One day, the surveyor happened to walk through the waiting room just as one waiting patient was reading the questions aloud to the rest of the waiting patients, who were then essentially "voting" on what answer should be selected. The resultant answers essentially represented a consensus of those available in the waiting room at that time rather than the opinions or behaviors of the person completing the questionnaire. Needless to say, the surveyor quickly changed his mode of administering questionnaires to a system that allowed for greater control over the number and identity of the persons completing the questionnaire. Unfortunately, when questionnaires are mailed, the surveyor has no way of checking up on such issues and must accept completed questionnaires "on faith."

Quick Turnaround

Earlier, we said that one of the advantages of using mail questionnaires is that the surveyor can assume that all of them were administered on the same date and that all respondents received the questionnaire on roughly the same date. In general, this means that data collected by mail will be more quickly completed than data collected in telephone or in-person interviews. There are exceptions to this, however. Generally, it takes a minimum of 2 weeks after each mailing for completed questionnaires to be returned to the surveyor. To the extent that the surveyor tries to maximize a good response rate by using **follow-up mailings** and telephone calls, the data collection period may extend to 2 or 3 months. (To our knowledge, there is no information currently available regarding the length of time most online surveys are kept available, and, as we have noted, no systematic efforts to conduct follow-ups have been reported.)

In contrast to the turnaround time required for mail surveys, it is possible to conduct a telephone survey literally "overnight" if the surveyor has the resources necessary to hire a large number of interviewers and the necessary number of telephones, *and* if the surveyor is willing to sacrifice a certain representativeness of the sample obtained. If, for example, all data are collected in one night from a sample of 500 persons, it clearly means that persons not at home that night have no chance of being in the sample. Also, persons whose lines are busy at the time of the initial attempted call are not likely to be in the sample, because, unlike regular telephone surveys, little or no redialing is done in such a survey.

For interviews about fast-breaking events, such as the destruction of the World Trade Center in New York City on September 11, 2001, a quick telephone survey or online survey is the only way to measure rapidly changing opinions. Both approaches, however, suffer from the lack of representativeness in the samples.

Self-Administered Questionnaires by Example: Assault and Vision Studies

In the remainder of this book, we explain and describe how self-administered questionnaires are developed and administered, using two actual studies as examples. The questionnaire used in the first study, the Workplace Assault Study, examined the extent to which the members of two locals of the Service Employees International Union (SEIU) perceived their workplace sites as safe, the incidence of physical assaults experienced while at work during the preceding year, and the incidence of threats of assault within the past month. Questionnaires were sent by mail to the homes of a stratified random sample of 1,744 potential respondents on January 17, 1995 (for more information on stratified random sampling, see **How to Design Survey Studies** and **How to Sample in Surveys**, Volumes 6 and 7 in this series).

The questionnaire used in the second study examined respondents' visual functioning, satisfaction, and experiences with side effects following radial keratotomy, a surgical procedure in which slices are made in the patient's cornea to reduce myopia, or nearsightedness. The questionnaire used in this study was administered as part of the 10-year follow-up examination in the Prospective Evaluation of Radial Keratotomy (PERK) Study, a multisite clinical trial of the 435 respondents who entered the study. In this study, question-naires were administered at one of the nine clinical sites by clinic coordinators (for more information on clinical trials and other survey designs, see **How to Design Survey Studies** and **How to Sample in Surveys**).

To reflect the normal progress and problems often associ-ated with the design of data collection instruments, in the following chapters we discuss what worked, what did not work, and what could have been improved in our two ques-tionnaires. Although most of our examples are drawn from these two studies, we also present examples drawn from other studies where appropriate.

2 Content of the Questionnaire

We begin this chapter by describing briefly the types of data surveyors can collect using questionnaires and how surveyors should make decisions regarding the appropriateness of using mail or electronic questionnaires. The remainder of the chapter focuses on the development of the content of the questionnaire.

Types of Data Collected Using Questionnaires

Studies of people generally collect data in one or more of five areas: (a) personal information about respondents (or **demographic data**), (b) information about respondents' environments, (c) information about respondents' behaviors, (d) information about respondents' experiences or status, and (e) information about respondents' thoughts or feelings. Some studies also focus on people's knowledge, attitudes, and behaviors. One of the worst things that can happen to a surveyor is to discover, in preparing to analyze the data, that the survey has failed to collect an essential piece of information. Inexperienced surveyors often forget to collect data on one or more important demographic variables, such as age, gender, education, occupational status, ethnic or racial identification, religious affiliation, or marital status. (For more on demographic data, see **How to Ask Survey Questions,** Volume 2 in this series.)

The other four types of data noted above, alone or in combination, usually form the focus of the research question. In the Workplace Assault Study, for example, we asked respondents about their experiences (specifically, about whether they had been assaulted or threatened) and their work environment, and we also asked them to provide demographic information (their genders, ages, and the types of jobs they do). We hypothesized that reports of assaults and threats would be associated with the workplace environment and possibly certain demographic characteristics.

Appropriateness of Using Mail or Electronic Questionnaires

Surveyors must evaluate three kinds of information in assessing whether or not they should attempt to collect data using mail or other self-administered questionnaires: the literacy level of the targeted population, the motivation level of the targeted population, and the amenability of the research question to data collection using a self-administered questionnaire.

LITERACY

In Chapter 1, we pointed out that self-administered questionnaires can be used only with literate respondents who are assumed to be highly motivated about the topic being studied. We have used mail questionnaires to study undergraduate and graduate alumni of UCLA. Clearly, such respondents meet the criterion of being literate. In contrast, mail questionnaires would not be a good means of studying participants in the Women, Infants, and Children's (WIC) supplemental feeding programs. WIC participants must meet a "means test" to qualify for the program. In California in 1994, the cutoff for participation was 185% of the poverty level. This meant that the annual income for a family of four could not exceed $27,380. Because income is correlated with education, a substantial number of the women enrolled in the WIC program have not completed high school, and many must be assumed to be functionally illiterate. Thus self-administered or mail questionnaires would not be a good way to collect information from WIC participants.

MOTIVATION

Much more difficult to determine than literacy is whether a target population is motivated to answer the questionnaire. Certainly, when members of a group decide they need to find out something about themselves, that is a good indication that group members are motivated to participate as respondents. For example, in the Workplace Assault Study, we knew that union members had expressed concerns about their vulnerability to assault and had sought out methods by which they could do a needs assessment.

Another indicator of the motivation of potential respondents is the amount of loyalty that individuals have to the group being studied. This criterion of loyalty suggests that mail and electronic questionnaires can be administered more successfully to identifiable groups—for example, alumni of UCLA, members of a professional organization, members of a church—than to general populations.

A strong appeal conveyed in the cover letter that accompanies a mail questionnaire can also serve to motivate compliance. We discuss the development of a cover letter in Chapter 4.

AMENABILITY OF THE RESEARCH QUESTION

A research question that is amenable to study using a self-administered questionnaire has four characteristics. First, the topic must be *contained*—that is, it must be one that can reasonably be covered in a relatively short and focused questionnaire instrument. This usually means that the study has a single objective and all the "sections" of the questionnaire interrelate and work together to achieve that objective. In the Workplace Assault Study, for example, the focus was exclusively on assault in the workplace. We were not trying to find out about assaults in nonworkplace environments, nor were we trying to find out other things about the workplace—for example, whether the respondents considered their jobs boring or challenging, why they chose their particular jobs, or even how long they had worked at their jobs.

Second, self-administered questionnaires generally work best when the focus of the research question is in the present. What are respondents doing *now?* What do they know *now?* How do they feel *now?* In the Workplace Assault Study, we were not trying to find out the respondents' employment histories or how and why they selected their particular career paths. Rather, we were asking respondents about what happened to them in the previous year (e.g., Were they assaulted?) and in the previous month (e.g., Were they threatened?). Our hope was that the respondents' concerns about vulnerability to assault would result in their being highly motivated and therefore increase their willingness to complete a questionnaire that asked them to remember events in the not-too-distant past. In other words, we were assuming that the salience of the topic would be sufficiently motivating to overcome certain other characteristics of the study that would usually argue against the use of a mail questionnaire.

Third, the research question must be such that the surveyor can structure the questionnaire so that, ideally, everyone answers every question. A surveyor can do this in one of two ways. The better of the two is to create response lists for *every* question that include responses that will enable all members of the sample to describe themselves. Surveyors sometimes accomplish this by including what is essentially a "not applicable" category in every set of response choices.

For example, in our study of vision and how people use their eyes, we *failed* to allow for such a possibility in one question. The question read as follows:

> When during the day do you usually
> read for pleasure?
>
> Morning 1
> Afternoon 2
> Evening 3

This question should have had a fourth alternative answer: "Never read for pleasure" (coded 4). The inclusion of such a response would have allowed persons who never read for pleasure to describe themselves. The omission of such an alternative increases the risk that respondents will get frustrated with the questionnaire because they feel that their behaviors or opinions are not sufficiently represented among the answer categories presented; as a result, they may not complete the questionnaire or may fail to return it. (In creating questionnaires for online surveys, surveyors must always remember to include a "not applicable" category in each set of response choices, because most of the software programs used to administer these questionnaires require the respondent to answer one question before he or she is allowed to go on to the next.)

Alternatively, surveyors can use skips or branching to increase their questionnaires' applicability to all potential respondents, although the use of such techniques should be minimized in self-administered questionnaires. For example, when we designed the questionnaire for the Workplace Assault Study, we knew that assault is a "rare event," and we did not expect many people in our study to say that they were assaulted within the past year, *even though many of them perceived themselves to be at risk of assault.* Consequently, we *had to* use branching or skip instructions in the questionnaire. We therefore formatted the first question as follows:

1. How many times have you been physically attacked or assaulted at work within the past year—that is, since October 1993?

RECORD NUMBER HERE

IF 0 ATTACKS IN PAST YEAR, SKIP TO
QUESTION 24 ON PAGE 7.

Persons who had been attacked within the past year answered 22 questions that asked them to describe various things about the attack. Persons who had not been attacked—the majority of respondents—skipped over this set of questions.

Similarly, Question 24 asked about threats within the past month. Again, we did not expect many people to report threats, so the questionnaire instructed those who had not received any threats to skip to Question 43.

24. **Within the past month**—that is, in the past 30 days—how many times have you been physically threatened or harassed?

RECORD NUMBER HERE

IF 0 THREATS IN PAST YEAR, SKIP TO
QUESTION 43 ON PAGE 13.

Those who had been threatened in the past month answered a series of questions; those who had not been threatened were instructed to skip to questions about demographic characteristics.

In this particular study, our use of two skips or branchings worked. But note that both of the skips were of a single kind: A person either answered a set of questions or skipped over a set of questions. Respondents were *not* asked to go to *different* sections of the questionnaire according to the answers they gave on a screening question. Furthermore, we restricted the number of skips included in the questionnaire to two. The general rule is this:

SKIPS SHOULD BE AVOIDED IN SELF-ADMINISTERED QUESTIONNAIRES.

If skips *must* be used, their use should be minimal and should *not* result in multiple branching operations, with one group of respondents being directed to one part of the questionnaire, a second group directed to another part, and a third group directed to yet another part. Respondents generally will *not* follow such instructions correctly and will be irritated by being asked to expend the effort to try to follow them. Thus a study of a general population's use of health services in which respondents vary in both age and gender is *not* amenable to study using paper and pencil self-administered questionnaires, because of the wide variety of types of services used and because the frequency of use by males and females and by people in different age groups varies substantially. A surveyor would have to use far too many skips in a questionnaire to provide appropriate questions for the various subgroups in the population.

As we noted in Chapter 1, some software packages for online surveys can handle skips and or branching in the questionnaire automatically. However, even when surveyors use programs that make skip patterns invisible to respondents, they should design their questionnaires as simply as possible, to minimize human errors in the notation or programming of the logical sequence of questions to be asked.

Fourth, self-administered questionnaires, and particularly mail questionnaires, are not appropriate for use in **exploratory studies**—that is, studies in which the research questions and the procedures by which those questions will be studied are still being developed. Surveyors should use mail questionnaires only when they have clear ideas about their research objectives and the parameters of their studies.

During the developmental stages of a study, the researcher should collect data in ways that maximize flexibility and the ability to pursue interesting topics that may or may not be central to the original question posed. Productive methods of collecting data in the early stages of a research project include the use of focus groups and semi-structured in-person interviews, in which the researcher can ask a lot of open-ended questions and has the ability to probe respondents' answers; observation; and even the collection of certain kinds of secondary data. Once the boundaries of the research question are clearly delineated, and assuming the question can appropriately be operationalized in a self-administered questionnaire (e.g., the sample is literate and motivated), then the surveyor can make the decision to use a self-administered questionnaire to collect the data.

Checklist: Deciding Whether to Use a Mail Questionnaire

✓ Respondents are literate and can answer all questions.

✓ Respondents are motivated.

- They want to know the information that the study is designed to gather.

- They feel part of a group that has reason to want the information.

✓ The topic is amenable to study using a self-administered questionnaire.

- The research objective is contained and focused.

- The research question asks about the present rather than the past or future.

- The questions in the questionnaire can be written so that they can be answered by everyone in the sample.

- The questionnaire can be constructed to avoid skips or branchings.

- The study is not exploratory or in the process of being developed.

Developing the Content of the Questionnaire

Once the surveyor determines that it is appropriate to use a self-administered questionnaire to collect data, his or her first task is to conduct a thorough search of the relevant or related literature. This **literature search** helps the surveyor refine the parameters of the data collection. What other studies have been done on this topic? How were the data collected in other studies? What was the content of the data collection instruments used in other studies of this topic? How can the surveyor learn from or build on these other research efforts? In developing our study on assault in the workplace, for example, we reviewed studies on occupational injury and found out three things:

1. Most studies on workplace injury had focused on deaths that occur on the job, with particular attention to homicides.

2. Most previous studies had used secondary data sets, such as coroners' or medical examiners' reports, death certificates, or official reports made to organizations such as the Occupational Safety and Health Administration. Needless to say, studies based on such sources tend to concentrate on the most serious occupational injuries—those that result in death or injuries sufficient to be reported to medical or other authorities.

3. The few studies that had *not* depended on secondary data sources or focused on severe injury or death had been concerned with injuries that occurred to staff (usually nurses) in institutional settings (usually psychiatric wards).

Knowledge of this literature and what it encompassed allowed us both to define how our study would build on or extend existing work in the area and to identify the data collection instruments that we should examine in deciding how to go about our study. Specifically, our study extended earlier research by assessing the frequency with which assaults *that are never recorded in official records* occur on the job and by expanding the occupational groups studied *beyond those working in locked institutional psychiatric hospitals*. Once we had completed the literature review, we knew which studies had used questionnaires to collect data, and we knew that in most cases self-administered questionnaires had been used. We then made every effort to obtain copies of all the earlier questionnaires *as they were actually administered to respondents*. We did *not* depend on the descriptions of the questionnaires that appeared in published articles or project reports.

ADOPTING STANDARD QUESTION BATTERIES

Ideally, we would have liked to find sets of questions that had already been developed and widely used and then simply **adopt** those questions as written. There are multiple advantages to this strategy of adopting **standard question batteries,** particularly for surveyors who are preparing mail questionnaires. First, such question batteries are almost always made up exclusively of closed-ended questions (as we noted in Chapter 1, respondents are generally reluctant to answer open-ended questions in self-administered questionnaires), and the possible answer categories have already been worked out and tested in prior studies. Second, the instructions to respondents have been developed and tested. And third, surveyors who use questions in a standard battery *exactly* as they were used in other studies can then compare the data they collect with the data collected in those prior studies or with a standard population. For example, many surveyors choose to ask questions about ethnicity or race exactly as they are asked in the U.S. Census form. They make this decision not because they think the U.S. Census has the "perfect" method for asking such questions, but because they want to be able to compare their own samples to the populations in particular regions. Figure 2.1 displays a portion of the 1990 U.S. Census form that includes questions (4 and 7) aimed at determining race and ethnicity. Using questions exactly as they were worded in the 1990 Census would allow a researcher to compare the race and ethnic distribution of his or her study sample with a "standard" population—namely, the population surveyed by the U.S. Census. Now that the 2000 U.S. Census is available for comparison, researchers are using questions as they were asked in that census. Figure 2.2 displays the portion of the 2000 U.S. Census form that includes questions (5 and 6) on race and ethnicity.

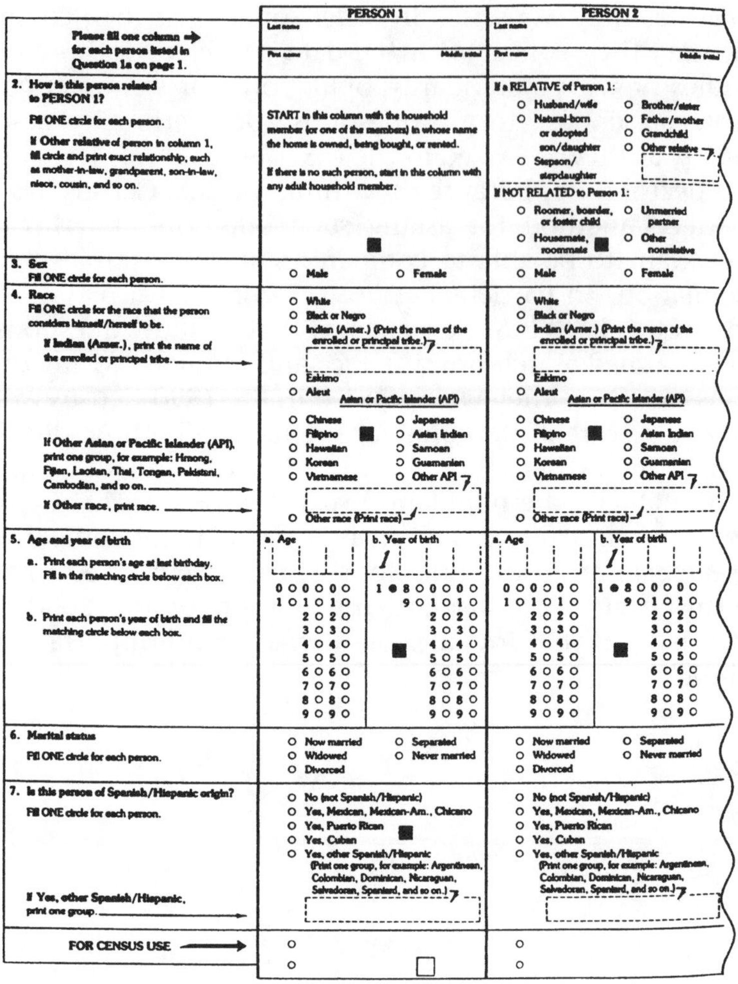

PERSON 1 — Last name / First name / Middle initial

PERSON 2 — Last name / First name / Middle initial

Please fill one column → for each person listed in Question 1a on page 1.

2. How is this person related to PERSON 1?
Fill ONE circle for each person.
If Other relative of person in column 1, fill circle and print exact relationship, such as mother-in-law, grandparent, son-in-law, niece, cousin, and so on.

Person 1: START in this column with the household member (or one of the members) in whose name the home is owned, being bought, or rented.
If there is no such person, start in this column with any adult household member.

Person 2: If a RELATIVE of Person 1:
O Husband/wife O Brother/sister
O Natural-born or adopted son/daughter O Father/mother
O Grandchild
O Other relative
O Stepson/stepdaughter
If NOT RELATED to Person 1:
O Roomer, boarder, or foster child O Unmarried partner
O Housemate, roommate O Other nonrelative

3. Sex
Fill ONE circle for each person.
O Male O Female

4. Race
Fill ONE circle for the race that the person considers himself/herself to be.
If Indian (Amer.), print the name of the enrolled or principal tribe. →
If Other Asian or Pacific Islander (API), print one group, for example: Hmong, Fijian, Laotian, Thai, Tongan, Pakistani, Cambodian, and so on. →
If Other race, print race. →

O White
O Black or Negro
O Indian (Amer.) (Print the name of the enrolled or principal tribe.)
O Eskimo
O Aleut
Asian or Pacific Islander (API)
O Chinese O Japanese
O Filipino O Asian Indian
O Hawaiian O Samoan
O Korean O Guamanian
O Vietnamese O Other API
O Other race (Print race)

5. Age and year of birth
a. Print each person's age at last birthday. Fill in the matching circle below each box.
b. Print each person's year of birth and fill the matching circle below each box.

a. Age — b. Year of birth 1

0 O 0 O 0 O — 1 ● 8 O 0 O 0 O
1 O 1 O 1 O — 9 O 1 O 1 O
2 O 2 O — 2 O 2 O
3 O 3 O — 3 O 3 O
4 O 4 O — 4 O 4 O
5 O 5 O — 5 O 5 O
6 O 6 O — 6 O 6 O
7 O 7 O — 7 O 7 O
8 O 8 O — 8 O 8 O
9 O 9 O — 9 O 9 O

6. Marital status
Fill ONE circle for each person.
O Now married O Separated
O Widowed O Never married
O Divorced

7. Is this person of Spanish/Hispanic origin?
Fill ONE circle for each person.
If Yes, other Spanish/Hispanic, print one group. →
O No (not Spanish/Hispanic)
O Yes, Mexican, Mexican-Am., Chicano
O Yes, Puerto Rican
O Yes, Cuban
O Yes, other Spanish/Hispanic (Print one group, for example: Argentinean, Colombian, Dominican, Nicaraguan, Salvadoran, Spaniard, and so on.)

FOR CENSUS USE →

Figure 2.1. Portion of the 1990 U.S. Census Form

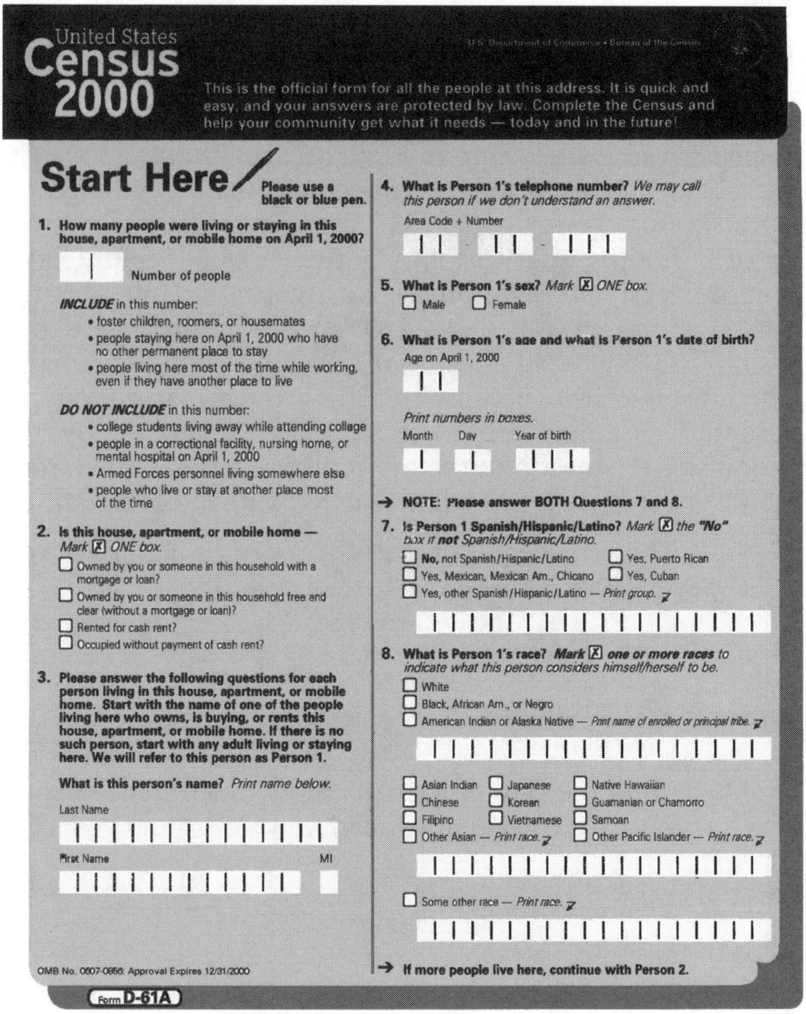

United States
Census 2000

U.S. Department of Commerce • Bureau of the Census

This is the official form for all the people at this address. It is quick and easy, and your answers are protected by law. Complete the Census and help your community get what it needs — today and in the future!

Start Here **Please use a black or blue pen.**

1. How many people were living or staying in this house, apartment, or mobile home on April 1, 2000?

Number of people

INCLUDE in this number:
- foster children, roomers, or housemates
- people staying here on April 1, 2000 who have no other permanent place to stay
- people living here most of the time while working, even if they have another place to live

DO NOT INCLUDE in this number:
- college students living away while attending college
- people in a correctional facility, nursing home, or mental hospital on April 1, 2000
- Armed Forces personnel living somewhere else
- people who live or stay at another place most of the time

2. Is this house, apartment, or mobile home — *Mark ☒ ONE box.*
- ☐ Owned by you or someone in this household with a mortgage or loan?
- ☐ Owned by you or someone in this household free and clear (without a mortgage or loan)?
- ☐ Rented for cash rent?
- ☐ Occupied without payment of cash rent?

3. Please answer the following questions for each person living in this house, apartment, or mobile home. Start with the name of one of the people living here who owns, is buying, or rents this house, apartment, or mobile home. If there is no such person, start with any adult living or staying here. We will refer to this person as Person 1.

What is this person's name? *Print name below.*

Last Name

First Name MI

4. What is Person 1's telephone number? *We may call this person if we don't understand an answer.*

Area Code + Number

5. What is Person 1's sex? *Mark ☒ ONE box.*
- ☐ Male ☐ Female

6. What is Person 1's age and what is Person 1's date of birth?

Age on April 1, 2000

Print numbers in boxes.

Month Day Year of birth

→ **NOTE: Please answer BOTH Questions 7 and 8.**

7. Is Person 1 Spanish/Hispanic/Latino? *Mark ☒ the "No" box if **not** Spanish/Hispanic/Latino.*
- ☐ **No,** not Spanish/Hispanic/Latino
- ☐ Yes, Puerto Rican
- ☐ Yes, Mexican, Mexican Am., Chicano
- ☐ Yes, Cuban
- ☐ Yes, other Spanish/Hispanic/Latino — *Print group.*

8. What is Person 1's race? ***Mark ☒ one or more races*** *to indicate what this person considers himself/herself to be.*
- ☐ White
- ☐ Black, African Am., or Negro
- ☐ American Indian or Alaska Native — *Print name of enrolled or principal tribe.*
- ☐ Asian Indian
- ☐ Japanese
- ☐ Native Hawaiian
- ☐ Chinese
- ☐ Korean
- ☐ Guamanian or Chamorro
- ☐ Filipino
- ☐ Vietnamese
- ☐ Samoan
- ☐ Other Asian — *Print race.*
- ☐ Other Pacific Islander — *Print race.*
- ☐ Some other race — *Print race.*

→ **If more people live here, continue with Person 2.**

OMB No. 0607-0856: Approval Expires 12/31/2000

Form D-61A

Figure 2.2. Portion of the 2000 U.S. Census Form

In other situations, surveyors adopt a question or set of questions because they want to compare respondents across samples. The Prospective Evaluation of Radial Keratotomy (PERK) Study was a clinical trail for which people volunteered because they were myopic (nearsighted) and wanted radial keratotomy, a surgical procedure that reduces myopia. Because study participants were "volunteers," we were interested in finding ways to compare these myopic volunteers to a more representative sample of myopes. In our literature search, we found out that RAND's Health Insurance Experiment (HIE) included a series of questions that asked people about their vision.[1] Because the HIE was done on a more representative sample and data had been collected by self-administered questionnaire, we replicated, or adopted, some of the vision questions exactly as used by RAND. For example:

43. During the **past 3 months**, how much pain have your eyes caused you? Would you say:

   A great deal of pain 1
   Some pain 2
   A little pain 3
   No pain at al. 4

44. During the **past 3 months**, how much have eyesight problems worried or concerned you? Would you say:

   A great deal 1
   Somewhat 2
   A little 3
   Not at all 4

45. During the **past 3 months**, how much of the time have eyesight problems kept you from doing the kinds of things other people your age do?

   All of the time 1
   Most of the time 2
   Some of the time 3
   A little of the time 4
   None of the time 5

Our inclusion of these three questions in the PERK question-naire allowed us to compare the PERK volunteers' percep-tions of their eyes to those of a more representative group of myopes. What we discovered was that PERK volunteers did *not* perceive themselves as having had more pain than RAND myopes, but *did* perceive themselves as being more disabled by their vision than RAND myopes. To that extent, the PERK volunteers "differed from" a more representative group of myopes.

Surveyors also use existing sets of questions exactly as they have been used before for two other reasons. First, many questionnaires—particularly those developed in the psychological literature—are protected by copyright. Copyright protection assures the authors of questionnaires that others cannot use or change their instruments without their permission. In the PERK Study, we used the SF-36 to measure the physical and mental health status of our sub-jects. The SF-36 was developed over a number of years under the auspices of RAND's Health Insurance Experiment. It therefore has the second characteristic that encourages sur-veyors to use existing questionnaires exactly as written: The validity and reliability of the items have been tested exten-sively over time and with different sample populations.

In our opinion, the SF-36 was the best measure available for assessing the concept of health status. Furthermore, it had the advantage that most of the development work on the instrument was done within the context of self-adminis-tered questionnaires. As a result, it was particularly relevant for use in the PERK Study, where subjects were asked to com-plete questionnaires at clinical sites. The existence of the copyright assures the authors of the SF-36 that other researchers will not use the instrument or make changes in it without requesting permission from them to do so. In some cases, researchers must pay fees in order to obtain permission to use copyrighted questionnaires; in all cases, researchers must give credit to and cite appropriately the persons who developed and tested the questions used.

ADAPTING SETS OF QUESTIONS

Unfortunately, many surveyors think that it is okay simply to select and use some questions from existing instruments. Neophyte surveyors and persons developing self-administered questionnaires are particularly prone to fall into this trap because of their eagerness to be able to say to potential respondents that "it will only take 5 minutes to fill out this questionnaire." Occasionally, a questionnaire that obtains valid and reliable data *can* be completed in 5 minutes, but this usually means that the questions have gone through extensive development and **pretesting** and that the topic under study is very tightly defined and presented. It usually takes respondents more than 5 minutes to provide thoughtful and complete information.

Surveyors do sometimes **adapt** or change existing instruments for use in their questionnaires, but they must be aware that when they do this, they can no longer reference prior psychometric testing of the instruments they have adapted, nor can they make direct comparisons between their samples and those to whom the original instruments were administered.

Surveyors usually adapt existing questionnaires for one of four reasons:

- They cannot use the existing questionnaires in their entirety because they are too long.

- They are studying populations other than the original populations for which the existing questionnaires were designed.

- They need to translate the existing instruments into other languages.

- They need to expand, reorder, or otherwise elaborate on items or change the procedures by which data are collected (e.g., an item written for an in-person interview may be modified for a mail questionnaire).

When surveyors modify existing instruments, they need to pilot-test the new versions as well as evaluate the reliability and validity of those versions.

For example: After due consideration, the members of a survey team decide to use an existing measure of health status, but they believe that they simply cannot afford for their questionnaire to include the complete measure, because that would make it too long; also, the questionnaire they are developing must operationalize multiple concepts, and health status is not the major focus of the study. The surveyors should not come to this conclusion without first pretesting their questionnaire with the complete health status measure and clearly demonstrating (a) that the questionnaire is too long in its original version and must be shortened and (b) that health status is a concept that is not of primary importance to testing the research question. Once they have done this, how should they proceed?

The surveyors' first step should be to contact the authors of the health status instrument and request their permission to select only certain items for use in the questionnaire. The surveyors should also ask the authors for advice on which items might be best suited to their proposed study. If the instrument is under copyright and the surveyors learn that the authors will not allow them to select items out of the battery to use in subsets, then they must find another measure of health status. Even if the questionnaire the surveyors want to adapt is not under copyright, they have a responsibility to respect the advice of the instrument's authors. If the authors agree that the surveyors can make modifications, then the surveyors have a responsibility to document carefully any changes they make and to state the reasons for the changes in any reports of their survey findings, where they must also acknowledge the source of the original questionnaire. In addition, the surveyors need to test the validity and reliability of the adapted questions.

EXAMPLE 2.1
Adapting the SF-36 in the PERK Study

In the PERK Study, we faced a problem. Volunteers for the study were originally enrolled in the study in the early 1980s. Upon entry to the study, each was asked to complete a questionnaire. We wanted to include a measure of health status in that questionnaire, and we talked to surveyors at RAND about using items from the Health Insurance Experiment questionnaire. Because data from the HIE were being analyzed at the time, they suggested that we use a subset of items that seemed to be "best" at that stage of their analyses. Subsequent analyses of the HIE data and other data sets ultimately resulted in the development of the SF-36 as a short form of the HIE's original measure of health status. Only some of the items in the original PERK questionnaire ended up in the SF-36.

As a result, when we designed the 10-year follow-up questionnaire for PERK patients, we decided that we needed to incorporate *both* the complete SF-36 *and* the items that were not included in the final SF-36 but that had been used in PERK's baseline and subsequent questionnaires. The inclusion of both sets of items meant that we could make two sets of comparisons. First, we could compare the health status of PERK volunteers at 10 years with other, more representative samples of the U.S. population; and second, we could compare the health status of PERK volunteers at 10 years with themselves at baseline and earlier follow-up periods.

We adapted both sets of items and lengthened the self-administered questionnaire. Thus at the analysis stage we had to complete new psychometric analyses, and during data collection we ran the risk of having lengthened the questionnaire either unnecessarily or detrimentally.

DESIGNING NEW QUESTIONS

We recommend that, whenever possible, surveyors either adopt or adapt questions from other studies. We think this is particularly important for self-administered questionnaires, because surveyors using such questionnaires should be concerned with maximizing the clarity of the questions. Surveyors should take advantage of the fact that others have developed and tested questions that they can use to operationalize concepts important to their research questions. When surveyors adapt or adopt questions from other sources, research ethics demand that they document where the instruments were obtained and give credit to the original designers.

The following guidelines summarize the discussion above concerning when surveyors should adapt or adopt questions from existing instruments or create new questions.

Guidelines for Deciding on the Content of the Questionnaire

- Conduct a literature review to define the parameters of the study, learn what others have done, and learn what others recommend.

- Adopt standard questionnaires to maximize closed-ended questions, because the questions and instructions have already undergone development and testing, and because using such instruments allows for comparison of the data with other studies. Give proper credit to the persons who developed the questions and pay fees for permission to use the questions if required.

- Adapt questions from other studies if the original questionnaires are too long, the mode of adminis-

---

tration is different, a different population is being studied, or translations must be made. Pilot-test the new version and assess its reliability and validity. Also, give credit to the sources of the questions adapted and explain the reasons for adaptation.

- Develop new questions when you cannot find any existing sets of questions that you can appropriately adopt or adapt for the purposes of your study.

Note

1. RAND is a nonprofit institute located in Santa Monica, California, that seeks to improve public policy through research and analysis. Begun in 1971, the Health Insurance Experiment was one of the largest controlled experiments ever attempted. Over a 15-year period, 2,700 families were randomly enrolled in health insurance plans that ranged from free care to 95% coinsurance. The objectives of the experiment were to determine which medical services to cover and the extent of coverage, to develop techniques for measuring health incomes, and to assess quality of care and the fairness and feasibility of different cost-sharing plans.

3 User-Friendly Questionnaires and Response Categories

A self-administered questionnaire, more than any other type of questionnaire, must maximize user-friendliness. Surveyors designing self-administered questionnaires must be concerned with the construction of the questions as well as the construction of the response categories. They need to avoid the use of open-ended questions, and they should be careful to provide instructions for respondents that are both clear and sufficient. Finally, they need to make every effort to avoid projecting personal biases into the wording of questions and answer categories.

Construction of Questions

SHORT-AND-SPECIFIC FORMAT

Questions in a self-administered questionnaire should be as short as possible and specific rather than general in what they reference. In creating short, specific questions, surveyors need to follow the rules for constructing any kind of questionnaire. For example, they should be careful to avoid **double-barreled questions**—that is, questions that ask two things at once, such as "How would you rate your local police on courtesy and effectiveness?" or "How often do you see or hear from your children and grandchildren?" They should also avoid using long, run-on sentences such as the following:

When you think about the traveling you might do in the next year or so, do you think you will make arrangements to travel in the next year if you decide to go by cruise ship?

Some people like to go out to the movies, others like to rent movies on video, others like to watch movies on cable TV, and others do not like to watch movies in a theater, on video, or on TV at all. How do you feel?

Creating short, specific questions may mean asking multiple questions rather than a single question. In the Workplace Assault Study, we needed to find out about the respondent's work environment—including the hours that he or she worked. We originally designed a question that read as follows:

When do you work? _____

RECORD HOURS WORKED

During pretesting of the questionnaire, we discovered that this question was not precise enough for a variety of reasons—some respondents in our sample worked different work shifts, others had rotating shifts, not every respondent worked the same days of the week, and so on. In responding to this question, some respondents gave us both days of the week and hours worked, others simply gave us the time they normally arrived at work, and others simply skipped the question, apparently because they found it too vague. We revised this single question into a series of questions as follows:

1. What time do you usually arrive at work?

   _____ AM   PM
   RECORD TIME OF DAY

2. What time do you usually leave work?

   _____ AM   PM
   RECORD TIME OF DAY

3. What days of the week do you usually work?

   _____
   RECORD DAYS OF THE WEEK

4. How many hours a week do you usually work?

   _____
   RECORD NUMBER OF HOURS/WEEK

We should note that, in creating this set of questions, we did two things that we generally do *not* recommend: We used open-ended questions, and we used the adverb *usually,* which is considered a vague qualifier (we discuss vague qualifiers later in this chapter).

We had two justifications for creating open-ended questions in this situation. First, we did not judge the answers we were requesting of respondents to be burdensome, nor did they require respondents to write down a lot of information. Second, even in self-administered questionnaires, open-ended questions sometimes obtain better data and take up less space than closed-ended questions. Questions 1, 2, and 4 above request information that can be considered "continuous" or "interval" in nature. In the case of Questions 1 and 2, the responses can be coded using a 24-hour clock; the responses to Question 4 can be entered into the data set exactly as given by the respondent.

In contrast, creating closed-ended questions to obtain the same information would have been difficult. They would have had to include all the possible alternative responses and would have taken up a lot of space that could be better used to ask additional questions. The one possible exception is Question 3, which we might have been wiser to format as follows:

3. What days of the week do you usually work?

CIRCLE ALL THAT APPLY
Sunday 1
Monday 2
Tuesday 3
Wednesday 4
Thursday 5
Friday 6
Saturday 7

Clearly, this list of responses is **exhaustive** and **mutually exclusive.** Furthermore, it allows the respondent to circle any combination of the seven responses and, quite frankly, makes future data entry easier. However, if we had made lists for any of the other three questions, we would have had to provide far more than seven mutually exclusive alternatives. Because Question 3 was part of a set of four questions, we reasoned that it would be easier for respondents to use the same kind of answer format for all four questions, so we elected not to change to a different strategy in the middle of the set. Nonetheless, this was a judgment call on our part.

We used the word *usually* in this set of questions because of the wide variety of work schedules and sites represented in this study. Included among others surveyed were nurses, probation officers, sheriff's department employees, employees of the department of parks and recreation, and employees of the municipal courts. Many of these employees worked a standard 40-hour week, but others worked unusual hours and shifts. Nonetheless, most respondents did have a "usual" time of starting work and a "usual" time of leaving work. By including the word *usually,* we were able to communicate to respondents that we knew there might be variation in the days and hours they worked without taking up further space with this set of questions.

To summarize, our original question—although short— was not sufficiently precise. It did not give us a complete picture of the days and hours that the respondent worked. In this case, our solution was to develop multiple, more specific questions. In other cases, surveyors may find it necessary to add qualifications to some questions. An example of the latter situation occurred in the PERK Study. In a follow-up questionnaire at 6 years, respondents were asked, "What proportion of the time do you wear glasses or contact lenses?" There were two frequent kinds of reactions to this question: Some respondents wrote on the questionnaire, "Do you mean when we are awake?" or some other similar comment; and many others, because they did not wear lenses at all or needed lenses only for one eye, either provided us with that information or simply skipped the question.

Once we realized that the question did not allow some of our respondents to describe themselves adequately and accurately, we were in a position of not knowing how to interpret the data for respondents who skipped the question or who did not write in further information. We attempted to clarify and correct this question in two ways when we wrote the questionnaire administered at 10 years. First, we elaborated the question to read as follows:

24. What proportion of the time that you are **awake** do you wear glasses or contact lenses in *either or both* eyes?

Second, we developed a much more elaborate set of questions that asked respondents about the extent to which and the reasons for which they wore lenses, and the types of lenses worn. Thus, in this instance, we had to lengthen the question to make it sufficiently specific and precise.

Obviously, when it is necessary to lengthen a question, the surveyor must be clear about *why* this is being done and take care to avoid constructing an overly long question.

CARE IN THE USE OF VAGUE QUALIFIERS

We noted above an example of an instance in which we added the word *usually* to a question. Surveyors should generally try to avoid adverbs like *usually* when writing questions because such words mean different things to different people. For example, we could have asked Question 24 as follows:

24. When you are awake, do you **usually** wear glasses or contact lenses in **either or both eyes?**

    Yes 1
    No 2

The problem with using *usually* in this instance is that some people might understand *usually* to mean wearing glasses all or most of the time, whereas others might understand it to mean wearing glasses less than 50% of the time when they are awake. *Usually* works as a **vague qualifier** in this example; when combined with the answer categories provided, it results in imprecise information about respondents, and particularly about those who answer yes to this question. Our solution in this case was to ask respondents about the proportion of time they wore lenses. (We should note that the word *proportion* could also create difficulty for some respondents who may be unfamiliar with the word or may not understand it. Because this study's sample was literate and highly educated, we believed that respondents would understand the term and have no difficulty in providing appropriate answers.)

Unless the surveyor remains vigilant, any adverb is likely to be a vague qualifier. Whenever a surveyor writes a question or a series of response alternatives that contains an adverb, he or she should evaluate carefully whether the question precisely measures the concept under study.

CARE IN THE USE OF ABSTRACT TERMS AND JARGON

Surveyors must be particularly careful to minimize the use of **abstract terms** or **jargon** in self-administered questionnaires. When they must use such language, they should take care to be sure that respondents understand it. This is a caveat in all questionnaire construction, but it is particularly important in self-administered questionnaires, where there is no interviewer available to clarify or provide a definition of a term if a respondent appears confused or hesitant about answering a question containing the term.

For example, in the PERK Study, respondents were fairly sophisticated about their vision and about ophthalmology, so we knew that they would be likely to understand such terms as *myopia* and *radial keratotomy.* If, however, we wanted to ask questions about vision in a questionnaire directed to a general sample of the population, we could not assume that respondents would understand such terms. Instead of asking if they were myopic, we would ask them if they were nearsighted or if they had difficulty seeing things at a distance. Even in the PERK questionnaire, we never used the term *myopia;* instead, we asked respondents about their ability to see at a distance.

We had a somewhat different problem in the Workplace Assault Study. The major objective of the study was to assess the prevalence of physical assaults in the workplace; we were not interested in emotional or verbal assaults. At the same time, we could not be sure that all of our respondents would understand the word *assault.* So, in introducing the series of questions about physical assault, we provided respondents with a definition of physical assault. Our intent was to maximize the number of respondents who would understand the question in the way that we intended it. The introduction read as follows:

> In the next set of questions, we would like you to describe any physical assaults or attacks that you have experienced within the past calendar year (that is, since January 1994) while you were at work. By a physical assault or attack, we mean a situation where one or more persons intentionally hit you or touched you with some part of their body or with a weapon or an object.

The data collected in both the pretest and the actual study suggested that respondents understood the term *physical assault* in the way we intended.

Far more problematic was a section of the questionnaire that asked about physical threats. We could find no formal definition of *physical threat* that had been used consistently by researchers collecting official statistics or other data. To the extent that threats had been studied, surveyors had tended to create their own definitions. After substantial discussion, we decided *not* to define the term for our respondents. Instead, we considered that a secondary objective of our study would be to find out inductively what people thought constituted a "physical threat" and whether reports and perceptions of threat varied with job category, frequency of reported threats or assaults, perceptions of the work environment, demographic factors, or other characteristics of our respondents.

In deciding not to define physical threats for our respondents, we put an additional burden on them, in that they had to generate their own definitions. Some complained about this, and the fact that we did not define the term may have reduced our response rate. This case also provides an example of an area of research where an interview with follow-up probes would probably work better than a self-administered questionnaire. However, given that we did not have the resources to interview our respondents but considered perceptions of physical threat to be an important topic for study, we chose to keep the questions on physical threat in the questionnaire. Of course, we could have provided our respondents with a definition, but in so doing, we would likely have created a definition that was either too restrictive or too broad. In either case, it would have represented our own perception of "physical threat" rather than the range of perceptions represented across our respondents.

To understand this range better, we included an open-ended question for respondents who said they had been threatened in the past month, asking them to describe "**the most serious threat.**" It was our hope that their answers might help us generate a definition of physical threat for use in future studies.

We considered asking *all* respondents in the study to give us their definitions of the term *physical threat,* but we decided that that would be unnecessarily burdensome for those who had not, in their opinion, experienced recent threats. Furthermore, by restricting our request to those who reported actual threats, we felt the information we received would be more accurate. This decision does not, of course, allow for the possibility that persons who did *not* report threats have a higher threshold at which they perceive a verbal or physical action to *be* a threat. For example, Respondent A may tell us that he was threatened in the past month and describe an occasion when a frustrated client swore at him. In contrast, Respondent B, who was similarly sworn at within the past month, may not remember the incident or may not consider it a threat. Hence he does not report being threatened and, as a result, does not subsequently describe this incident to us.

To summarize: Surveyors should avoid using abstract terms and jargon in self-administered questionnaires as much as possible. If they do use such language, they should provide definitions. This may not be difficult if standard definitions are readily available in the literature, but it may be impossible if the terms that need to be defined come from relatively new areas of study. In the latter case, self-administered questionnaires may not be the best way of collecting the data. If surveyors must use undefined terms in their self-administered questionnaires, they should give the respondents an opportunity to explain what they understand the terms to mean. The surveyors may also have to decide whether to ask all respondents how they use the terms or only those who respond to particular questions in certain ways.

EASY-TO-DIFFICULT PROGRESSION

In designing all questionnaires, surveyors should try to start with the easiest questions and proceed to more complex or sensitive questions. Even though respondents to a mail questionnaire can decide to answer the items in any order they choose, this rule still holds. Indeed, it is possibly even more important for a mail questionnaire, in that the surveyor wants the first few pages of the questionnaire to look inviting, to encourage the respondent to participate in the study and answer all the questions asked. Even in online questionnaires it is important that the beginning questions be interesting, despite the fact that respondents cannot skip ahead. Surveyors conducting online surveys often find a substantial amount of abandonment among their returns—that is, respondents quit before completing the questionnaire. This may happen in part because they have placed difficult or nonstimulating questions too close to the beginning of the questionnaire.

In the 10-year follow-up for the PERK Study, we were particularly interested in the extent to which and the occasions on which respondents used glasses or contact lenses to see well, so a substantial part of the questionnaire focused on this topic. Figure 3.1 shows part of the sequence of questions asked. Notice that the first question asks whether the respondent currently wears glasses or contact lenses in either eye. We then go on to ask a general question about the *amount* of time lenses are worn. (Remember that eventually we ask respondents for more detailed information about the actual *proportion* of time they wear their lenses.) Questions 4 through 8, which are not included in Figure 3.1, ask further general questions about respondents' vision now and prior to their having radial keratotomy.

Since your last examination in the PERK Study, some patients have had a lot of changes in their lenses and the extent to which they need to wear lenses. Others have had no changes. The next set of questions asks about **your** experience with corrective lenses. (CIRCLE THE NUMBER THAT CORRESPONDS TO YOUR ANSWER.)

2. Do you currently wear glasses or contact lenses in **either** eye to improve your eyesight?

    Yes . . . . GO TO Q3 1
    No . . . . GO TO Q3 2
    No, but should wear lenses. . . . ANSWER A. 3

    A. Why don't you wear lenses and why should you wear lenses?

    _____

    _____

3. Do you wear these all the time or only sometimes?

    All the time . . . . ANSWER A. 1
    Only sometimes . . . . ANSWER A. 2
    Do not wear lenses . . . . GO TO Q4 3

    A. What are your **main** reasons for wearing corrective lenses?

    _____

    _____

9. Did anyone in the PERK Study ever tell you that **after** you had surgery you might have to wear glasses or other lenses for **reading** and other **close work?**

    Yes. 1
    No. 2

10. Has that happened to you? Do you **currently** wear reading glasses or lenses for:

    CIRCLE ALL THAT APPLY

    Left eye, ... 1
    Right eye, or 2
    Neither eye? 3

Figure 3.1a. Constructing and Ordering Questions From Easy to Difficult

11. **Following surgery** for radial keratotomy, when did you **first** start wearing reading glasses or lenses for one or both eyes?

CIRCLE ALL THAT APPLY

First started wearing reading lenses
in my right eye in: _____ / _____ 1
                   YEAR   MONTH

First started wearing reading lenses
in my left eye in: _____/_____ 2
                   YEAR   MONTH

Do not wear reading glasses or lenses. 3

12. Some people have reading glasses or lenses but do not need to wear them for all near tasks. Others need reading lenses for only one of their eyes. Please use the following list to describe your use of lenses for **near vision** on **each eye.**

I must use glasses or some other visual aid on my **RIGHT EYE** to:

	YES	NO
Read newspaper headlines.	1 . . .	2
Read newspaper articles.	1 . . .	2
Read telephone books	1 . . .	2
Read numbers on a microwave	1 . . .	2
Read my watch.	1 . . .	2
Read a computer screen.	1 . . .	2
Read in dim light.	1 . . .	2
Read in bright light	1 . . .	2
When my right eye is tired	1 . . .	2
Read a book in the morning when I get up.	1 . . .	2
Read a book in the evening	1 . . .	2
Thread a needle.	1 . . .	2
Other	1 . . .	2
SPECIFY: _____		
I use my right eye **without** a lens for near vision.	1 . . .	2
I **never** use a lens on my right eye for near vision	1 . . .	2

Figure 3.1b. Constructing and Ordering Questions From Easy to Difficult

I must use glasses or some other visual aid on my **LEFT EYE** to:

	YES	NO
Read newspaper headlines	1	2
Read newspaper articles	1	2
Read telephone books	1	2
Read numbers on a microwave	1	2
Read my watch	1	2
Read a computer screen	1	2
Read in dim light	1	2
Read in bright light	1	2
When my left eye is tired	1	2
Read a book in the morning when I get up	1	2
Read a book in the evening	1	2
Thread a needle	1	2
Other	1	2
SPECIFY: _____		
I use my left eye **without** a lens for near vision	1	2
I **never** use a lens on my left eye for near vision	1	2

Figure 3.1c. Constructing and Ordering Questions From Easy to Difficult

Starting with Question 9, the questions become more complex and require more thought. Because it has been hypothesized that persons who have had radial keratotomy might have to wear reading glasses sooner and for a greater number of activities than would comparably aged persons who have *not* had the surgery, it was important for us to obtain detailed information about the circumstances under which respondents had to wear glasses or contact lenses to see. It was also important to find out whether or not they remembered ever being told that they might have to wear lenses for close work.

Questions 9 and 10 are more difficult than Questions 2 and 3 in that they ask respondents about their use of lenses for particular activities—namely, close work and reading. But Questions 9 and 10 are significantly easier to answer than Questions 11 and 12. Question 11 requires respondents to use "retrospective memory"—in other words, to think back in time. If they are now wearing reading glasses, when did they start? In Question 12, respondents are provided with a list of tasks that may require the use of glasses and asked whether or not they wear lenses for each task.

Furthermore, respondents are asked to *differentiate between* their two eyes. Generally, we would not expect respondents to be able to make such detailed distinctions between their eyes without help from an interviewer. However, because these particular respondents had been enrolled in a vision study for more than 10 years, we knew they were substantially more sophisticated about their eyes than the average person, and so we were confident we would be able to obtain this information. Yet even with this sample we began with general questions and gradually progressed to more complex ones.

LOGICAL ORDER

Questions should be asked in **logical order.** One common error that beginning surveyors make is in ordering questions according to when they think about them instead of in some logical sequence. In the most extreme cases, they may even ask respondents to flip back and forth between topics. Figure 3.2 provides an example of this kind of error. Here we have two demographic questions (Questions 1 and 3), two questions about physical activity (Questions 2 and 5), and one question about health (Question 4). If these questions were asked in logical order, related questions would be grouped together. In other words, Questions 1 and 3 would be in sequence and would be placed with other demographic questions, Questions 2 and 5 would be together and placed with other questions about physical activities, and Question 4 should be placed with other questions about health status.

Figure 3.1 also illustrates the principle of putting questions in logical order. It makes no sense to ask respondents about the circumstances under which they wear glasses or contact lenses *before* asking them if they wear lenses at all. As

1. Are you currently employed at a regular job?

> Yes . . . . ANSWER A-B 1
> No . . . . GO TO Q2 2

A. What days of the week do you usually work?

_____

B. What hours do you usually work?

_____

2. About how often do you participate in sports or physical activities? Would you say:

> At least once a day. 1
> Less than once a day but several times a week 2
> 2-3 times a week 3
> Once a week 4
> Less than once a week. 5
> Never. 6

3. How old were you on your last birthday?   _____

> RECORD AGE

4. In general, would you say your health is:

> Excellent. 1
> Very good 2
> Good. 3
> Fair 4
> Poor. 5

5. When you participate in physical activities, about how long do you participate each time?

> _____
> RECORD # OF MINUTES
> DO NOT PARTICIPATE 999

Figure 3.2. Example of an Illogical and Poorly Ordered Questionnaire

Figure 3.1 shows, questions tend to be logically ordered when general questions are asked before more specific ones.

PLACEMENT OF DEMOGRAPHIC QUESTIONS

As we have noted above, questions should be grouped by topic area. This applies to demographic questions (questions about respondent characteristics such as age, gender, employment status, income, and marital status) as well as to questions related to the survey topic. However, surveyors differ in their opinions concerning *where* in the questionnaire demographic questions should be located.

We believe that demographic questions should be placed at the end of the questionnaire. We recommend this for three reasons. First, a mail questionnaire is almost always preceded by an introductory letter or statement that describes the subject matter of the study and encourages respondent participation. Whether such a letter is sent in advance or included with the questionnaire itself, its purpose is to intrigue respondents and encourage their participation in the study. If the first questions in the questionnaire are demographic ones, this tends to negate the positive influence of the introductory letter. Second, many people find demographic questions boring. By beginning with boring questions, the surveyor increases the probability that respondents will become disinterested in the study and never complete the questionnaire. Finally, many respondents consider the topics of some demographic questions, such as age and income, to be highly personal. Starting a questionnaire with questions that respondents are reluctant to answer reduces the probability that respondents will complete the questionnaire and return it to the surveyor.

Although it is true that a respondent can read an entire mail questionnaire before answering any of its questions, we still believe that starting a questionnaire with easy questions that immediately engage the respondent in the topic of a study will increase response rates and reduce the amount of missing data. Other surveyors disagree with this position and believe that it is best to ask demographic questions at the beginning of a questionnaire. Their reasons for this position are twofold: First, demographic questions are easy for respondents to answer because they know the information being sought; and second, putting demographic questions at the beginning maximizes the likelihood of getting complete demographic information, because those respondents who return incomplete questionnaires tend to leave the last part of the questionnaires unanswered. In our opinion, this latter argument—if operative—has more salience for questionnaires used in telephone or in-person interviews, where the interviewer controls the order in which questions are asked, than it does for self-administered questionnaires, where the order in which questions are answered ultimately rests with the respondent. Also, we suspect that if a respondent is not going to answer a substantial number of the questions in a questionnaire, he or she will very likely not even return the questionnaire to the surveyor.

Checklist for Constructing Questions

✓ Keep questions short.

✓ Make questions specific.

✓ Avoid vague qualifiers.

✓ Avoid abstract terms.

✓ Avoid jargon.

✓ Avoid **slang**.

✓ Start with easier questions and move to more difficult ones.

✓ Ask questions in a logical order.

✓ Decide *where* to place demographic questions and *why* you are choosing that location.

Open- Versus Closed-Ended Questions

Items in questionnaires can be either open-ended or closed-ended. Questions 2, 3, 10, 11, and 12 in Figure 3.1 and Questions 1, 2, and 4 in Figure 3.2 are examples of closed-ended questions. Questions 2A, 3A, and the dates in Figure 3.1 and Questions 1A, 1B, and 5 in Figure 3.2 are examples of open-ended questions. Open-ended questions have no lists of possible answers; closed-ended questions, however, include lists of **answer categories** (or **response categories**)— that is, possible answers from which respondents select the answer or answers that best represent their view or situation.

Although open-ended questions are much easier to write than closed-ended items, they generally are more difficult to answer, code, and analyze because surveyors must develop code frames or categories to organize and summarize the collected data. This process is sometimes referred to as *content analysis.* In contrast, closed-ended questions are much more difficult to design, but if designed carefully and with sufficient pretesting, they result in much more efficient data collection, processing, and analysis. With closed-ended questions, instead of having to write out (or, in the case of online surveys, type in) answers, the interviewer or respondent selects the words, phrases, or statements that best match the respondent's answer from the lists of answers provided. (In the case of online surveys, the response categories may appear on the screen as part of the text of the question or may appear in "dropdown menus" that are revealed when the respondent uses the mouse to click on the response area.)

As we noted in Chapter 1, surveyors should avoid using open-ended questions (or use them only sparingly) in mail and other self-administered questionnaires. Although neophyte surveyors may think that open-ended questions allow respondents to express themselves in greater detail and with greater accuracy, without being "forced" to choose among predetermined categories, in fact, respondents do not like to answer open-ended questions, in part because the physical process of writing out or typing answers is tiring. Open-ended questions also require respondents to generate their own answers without any prompting from the surveyor.

Note that in the examples displayed in Figures 3.1 and 3.2, we ask open-ended questions only in situations where the amount of writing demanded of a respondent is minimal, where it would have been impossible to generate a complete list of possible responses in advance (e.g., Question 2A in Figure 3.1), and where the open-ended questions follow dependent questions (that is, questions that are asked of only some respondents). For example, in Figure 3.2, only those respondents who answer yes to Question 1 are asked to answer Questions 1A and 1B; those who answer no to Question 1 skip these two open-ended questions.

Construction of Response Categories

Clearly, if self-administered questionnaires are dominated by closed-ended questions, the task of developing the response categories for such questions is particularly important. To be useful for gathering meaningful data, a list of response categories should have the following characteristics:

- The list should be exhaustive while simultaneously not being too long.

- The categories in the list should be mutually exclusive, and respondents should be able to distinguish the boundaries separating the categories easily.

- The list should be set up to allow respondents to provide multiple answers when relevant.

- When appropriate, the list should include a residual "other" category.

Generally, the lists of response categories in mail questionnaires should be shorter than the lists provided in interviewer-administered questionnaires. Surveyors designing self-administered questionnaires also need to keep in mind that their respondents will always see the full range of responses provided, whereas in interviewer-administered questionnaires, responses may be provided for the interviewer to use but *not* read to the respondent.

The advantage of having respondents see the response categories is that they are less likely to be influenced by either primacy or **recency effects.** In other words, instead of tending to select the first or the last response provided at the expense of all the other alternatives, respondents are more likely to pay attention to the entire list of responses. In general, people recognize and retain visual cues better than they do auditory cues, so if they see the list of responses, they are more likely to select the one that best represents them rather than the one that they best recall or most recently recall hearing.

The disadvantage of respondents' being able to see the list of possible responses is that they are less likely to volunteer answers that are not on the list, even if the available responses do not provide an adequate description of their behavior or feelings. If response alternatives are persistently too restrictive or too vague, respondents may become frustrated by their inability to describe themselves accurately. To the extent that frustration increases, response rates decrease. Thus it is extremely important that surveyors spend sufficient time developing and pretesting the response alternatives provided for each question in a self-administered questionnaire.

EASILY USED CATEGORIES

In the 10-year follow-up on the PERK Study, we wanted to find out about some of the common activities for which people use their eyes (e.g., reading, driving, and watching television). We wanted to know the extent to which they used their eyes in such activities, whether or not the amount of time they spent in such activities had changed over the past year, and when during the day they engaged in such activities. At the same time, we did not want to ask a large number of questions about these activities.

Figure 3.3 shows the series of questions we designed. Notice that neither Question 56 nor Question 60 provides an exhaustive list of answer categories. To accomplish that, we should have done two things: first, added a category that allowed for respondents to state that they "never read for pleasure"; and second, provided instructions that allowed for respondents to circle "all that apply." Question 56 is a good example of how vague qualifiers (which frequently are adverbs) can get a surveyor into trouble. Here, in using the word *usually,* we meant for respondents to indicate "when you mainly read for pleasure" or "when you do your major pleasure reading." Many of our respondents either circled multiple alternatives or wrote along the side of the question that they read for pleasure, for example, in both the morning and the evening. If a mail or other self-administered questionnaire contains too many questions with these kinds of problems, the average respondent eventually will get irritated and, as a result, may refuse to complete the questionnaire.

MUTUALLY EXCLUSIVE CATEGORIES

Notice that in Questions 54 and 55 in Figure 3.3, which ask about reading for pleasure, we attempted to incorporate answer categories that would allow us to assess both the current frequency with which people read and the extent to which reading patterns might have changed in the past year while *simultaneously* allowing response categories that would differentiate persons who no longer read for pleasure from those who never read for pleasure. We set up Questions 58 and 59 similarly to find out about driving and watching television.

Unfortunately, however, the last two alternatives in Question 54 were worded in such a way that they were neither clear nor mutually exclusive. In part, the confusion resulted from the fact that the present tense and past tense of the verb *read* are spelled the same way. Had we discovered the confusion during pretesting, we could have rewritten the response categories in Question 54 to be analogous to those

In the next set of questions we need to find out about some of your daily activities and how you spend your time.

54. Do you currently read magazines, books, and newspapers as much as you ever did, more than you did a year ago, less than you did a year ago, or don't you read for pleasure at all?

I read for pleasure:

Much more than a year ago 1
Somewhat more than a year ago 2
About the same as a year ago.............................. 3
Somewhat less than a year ago............................. 4
Do not read for pleasure at all 5
Never read for pleasure................................... 6

55. About how often do you read for pleasure?

Several times a day....................................... 1
At least once a day 2
Less than once a day but several times a week 3
2-3 times a week... 4
Once a week 5
Less than once a week 6
Never.. 7

56. When during the day do you usually read for pleasure?

Morning 1
Afternoon 2
Evening................... 3

57. When you read for pleasure, about how long do you read each time?

_____

RECORD # OF MINUTES

DO NOT READ FOR PLEASURE 999

Figure 3.3a.   Examples of Exhaustive and Mutually Exclusive Answer Categories

58. How often did you drive a car in the past week?

I never drove a car 1
I no longer drive a car 2
I did not drive in the past week 3
I drove 2-3 times 4
I drove several times 5
I drove every day 6

59. How often did you watch television in the past week?

I never have watched television 1
I no longer watch television 2
I did not watch TV in the past week 3
I watched TV 2-3 times 4
I watched TV several times 5
I watched TV every day 6

60. When, during the day, do you usually watch television?

Morning 1
Afternoon 2
Evening 3

61. When you watch television, about how long do you watch each time?

_____

RECORD # OF MINUTES

NEVER WATCH TELEVISION 999

Figure 3.3b. Examples of Exhaustive and Mutually Exclusive Answer Categories

used in Questions 58 and 59—for example, "I no longer read for pleasure" and "I have never read for pleasure."

MULTIPLE ANSWERS

Surveyors use two techniques in making response categories both flexible and exhaustive. The first is to set up response categories so that respondents can select more than one answer to describe themselves. In Figure 3.4, Questions 25 and 26 both allow respondents to select multiple answers. Although most physical attacks are committed by a single person with a single weapon, Question 25 asks the respondent how many people were involved in the attack, and Question 26 provides the respondent with an opportunity to describe multiple attackers in terms of the kinds and variety of roles they had relative to the respondent. Thus if a respondent reported in answer to Question 25 that he or she was attacked by three persons, the respondent might then go on in Question 26 to select three answers, such as "Patient/ client with whom I had worked," "Patient/client whom I did not know," and "Friends/relatives of a patient/client." Similarly, in Question 27, the respondent might report that both a chair and fists were used in the attack.

When the questionnaire makes provisions for respondents to give multiple answers, the surveyor must also make provisions for the multiple answers to be efficiently and completely coded into the data set for analysis. The easiest way to do that is to create a separate variable for each answer response provided and set up consistent codes for whether a given response is or is not selected or circled by the respondent. In the example questions shown in Figure 3.4, we might decide that circled responses would be coded 1 for "mentioned" and those not circled would be coded 2 for "not mentioned." (In online surveys, respondents typically are asked to click on boxes or "radio buttons" next to their answer choices, and those responses are recorded in the data file.) The responses for Question 26 would generate 10 differ-

22. Please describe the **most serious attack you had in the last year:**

_____

_____

23. When did this attack occur? _____ / _____ / _____

      MONTH   DAY   YEAR

24. What time of day did this attack occur? _____

      RECORD TIME OF DAY

25. Were you attacked by one person or more than one person?

      One person 1
      More than one person 2
      How many? _____

26. Who was the person(s) who attacked you?

      CIRCLE ALL THAT APPLY

      Patient/client with whom I had worked 1
      Patient/client whom I did not know 2
      Friends/relatives of a patient/client 3
      Co-worker/other employee 4
      Supervisor or boss 5
      Subordinate or person who works for me 6
      Former employee 7
      Person in legal custody 8
      General public/someone "off the street" 9
      Other 10
      Who? _____

27. Did the person(s) who attacked you have a weapon?

      CIRCLE ALL THAT APPLY

      Yes, a gun 1
      Yes, a knife 2
      Yes, an object 3
          What was the object? _____
      Yes, a chair or other piece of furniture 4
      They used their fists or body 5
      Other 6
          Please describe: _____

Figure 3.4.   Examples of Residual "Other" and Use of Multiple Response
               Categories

ent variables—one for each of the possible available categories provided. Similarly, the responses for Question 27 would generate 6 different variables.

For the respondent described above, the codes corresponding to the 10 variables created in response to Question 26 would be 1 for each of the variables that coordinate with "Patient/client with whom I had worked," "Patient/client whom I did not know," and "Friends/relatives of a patient/client" and 2 for each of the other 7 variables. For Question 27, a code of 1 would be recorded for each of the variables that correspond to "Yes, a chair or other piece of furniture" and "They used their fists or body" and 2 for each of the variables that correspond to "Yes, a gun," "Yes, a knife," "Yes, an object," and "Other."

RESIDUAL "OTHER" CATEGORY

The inclusion of a **residual "other" category** is the second technique surveyors can use to increase flexibility in answer categories. Both Questions 26 and 27 in Figure 3.4 include a residual "other." We consulted the literature and used information provided by focus groups and pretests in creating the lists of answer categories provided in Questions 26 and 27. In Question 26, we tried to create an exhaustive list of the different kinds of people who might attack members of Locals 535 and 660 of the Service Employees International Union. Because the two locals represent a wide variety of jobs, we needed to create a list that would be as exhaustive as possible and take into account the fact that, for example, psychiatric nurses and employees of the department of parks and recreation interact with different types of people and different mixes of people. A psychiatric nurse who works on a locked ward will spend a substantial part of his or her work time interacting with incarcerated persons. In contrast, an employee of the parks department will interact primarily with fellow workers.

In attempting to create an exhaustive list, we also needed to be careful not to make the list too long. And although we wanted the list to be detailed, we did not want it to be *too* detailed. For example, in Question 26, we combined "patients" with "clients." Once we had finished our pretest, we felt that our list was fairly exhaustive, but we could not be absolutely sure we had included all possibilities, so we added a residual "other." Thus if a respondent had been attacked by a type of person we had failed to include in our list of categories—for example, a member of the union staff—the respondent could circle 10, which corresponds to "other," and describe this person in the space provided.

Sometimes, respondents are unsure about which categories to use. For example, if a respondent works in the tax office and is attacked by someone who works down the hall for the courts, she may not consider the person who attacked her a "coworker or other employee." As a result, she would not circle 4 in response to Question 26; instead, she might circle 10 for "other" and describe the person in the space provided.

Once all the questionnaires have been returned, the surveyor must decide how to handle the residual "other" answers in data analysis. In each case, there are two choices: The surveyor can either move the volunteered answer into one of the existing variable categories or create a new—in the case of Question 26, 11th—variable that represents the new answer. In the two examples above regarding Question 26, we would create a new variable for the union employee but would consider the court worker to be a coworker or other employee, and so would recode that respondent's answer as 4.

The surveyor needs to apply two general rules in deciding whether or not to create a new category or variable from an answer recorded in the residual "other" category. First, he or she needs to determine how closely the answer given in the residual "other" category relates to answer categories already specified. In the above example, we suggest that a person who works in an office down the hall is appropriately considered a coworker but that a union employee constitutes a "different" category of person and thus necessitates the creation of a new answer category or variable. Second, the surveyor needs to examine the number of respondents who put particular answers into the residual "other" category. If, for example, we have a substantial number of respondents tell us that coworkers from offices down the hall had attacked them, we might well decide that the number of responses justifies the creation of two categories of coworkers: those who work within the same office and those who work in adjacent offices. The surveyor must make decisions concerning whether or not new categories and variables should be created during data entry.

In developing answer categories, surveyors should try to minimize the use of residual "other." If more than 10% of the respondents in our sample had used the residual "other" category to describe their attackers, we would have known that we probably had done insufficient thinking before creating our list of answer possibilities. When large numbers of respondents have to use the residual "other" category to answer any given question, the surveyor will have to post-code those data if they are to be meaningful. This is especially true for online surveys, where "other" category responses require respondents to type in their answers. Furthermore, when respondents find that the lists of responses provided for questions consistently do *not* allow them to describe themselves accurately, they will likely do one of two things: They will arbitrarily put themselves into a category simply because it is there and not because it accurately represents them, or they will become so frustrated by the questionnaire that they neither complete it nor return it.

Checklist for
Constructing Response Categories

✓ Avoid open-ended questions.

✓ Create exhaustive lists of responses.

✓ Keep answer alternatives short and precise.

✓ Create mutually exclusive answer categories.

✓ Decide for each question whether respondents should be restricted to a single response or allowed to provide multiple responses.

✓ Consider the need for a residual "other" answer category.

Clear and Sufficient Instructions

Clear instructions are important in any questionnaire, but they are particularly important in mail and other self-administered questionnaires because no interviewer is present to help the respondent understand the questions or how he or she should go about completing the questionnaire. Instructions in self-administered questionnaires can be classified into three types: general instructions, transitional instructions, and question-answering instructions.

GENERAL INSTRUCTIONS

Most questionnaires should include some set of **general instructions** as part of their introductory material. Figure 3.5 shows the instructions that appeared in the introduction to the PERK questionnaire. Notice that the instructions provide information about the kinds of questions that will be asked. Because we knew that respondents might find some of the questions repetitive, we also included a brief explanation of *why* such repetition occurs. The general instructions on any questionnaire should emphasize the fact that the surveyors are interested in the respondents' opinions, ideas, and experiences. This kind of information is particularly important when questionnaires are being distributed within an institutional site, such as a school, health clinic, or workplace, or when respondents may think that the answers they give will be used in providing them with access to services, jobs, or goods.

TEN-YEAR FOLLOW-UP QUESTIONNAIRE
Prospective Evaluation of Radial Keratotomy (PERK) Study
Psychosocial and Visual Characteristics

As part of the Prospective Evaluation of Radial Keratotomy (PERK) Study, we are interested in finding out about your current vision and some of your experiences since you were last examined in the PERK Study. This questionnaire includes questions about your current vision, your general health, your use of corrective lenses, and about any problems you might have had since we last examined you. Although we know that you may find some of the questions repetitive, please answer all of them. Questions are repeated so that we can compare your experiences and opinions now—10 years after your first surgery—with your experiences before surgery, immediately after surgery, and 6 years after surgery.

We are interested in **your** opinions, ideas, and experiences. All the information you provide is confidential and will be published **only** in summary, statistical form. You will not be identified in any way. In order to get accurate information about radial keratotomy and how it affects people's vision, we need information from **all** PERK patients. So please help us by answering the questions to the best of your ability.

Please fill out the entire questionnaire now. We have arranged for you to have enough time to finish the questionnaire before we start your vision testing. When you are **finished** with the questionnaire, **seal** the questionnaire in the attached envelope and **leave it with** the clinical coordinator for the PERK Study.

Figure 3.5.   Example of Instructions Used at the Beginning of a
Questionnaire

The general instructions should also state what the respondent is supposed to do with the questionnaire when he or she has completed it—for example, "seal the questionnaire in the attached envelope and leave it with the clinical coordinator." In the PERK Study, we developed this procedure because of our concern that respondents might think, because they were filling out the questionnaire in a clinic, that the ophthalmologist or other health personnel might have access to the questionnaire and thus know who completed it and that this access might in some way influence their health care—especially if they said something negative about the surgery or the clinical site. Surveyors can never be completely sure that such instructions will eliminate acquiescence bias (i.e., the need to please the surveyor), but they should attempt to address the possibility of this kind of bias by any means they can.

Finally, the general instructions should assure respondents that they will have sufficient time to complete the questionnaire. We added this information to the instructions in the PERK Study when we discovered that earlier in the study questionnaires had sometimes been given to patients who had just had dilating drops put in their eyes, which made it difficult for them to read the questionnaires, and some patients had been asked to complete questionnaires as they progressed through various ophthalmic tests.

Some questionnaires do not demand introductory instructions as elaborate as those illustrated in Figure 3.5. This is particularly true if **cover letters** are provided with the questionnaires or if respondents have received **advance letters.** For example, we did not provide lengthy general instructions in the Workplace Assault Study because we included both advance letters and cover letters in the study design. For an online survey that is being administered to a list sample, the surveyor may send informative advance letters or e-mail notices to potential respondents. When the surveyor does not specifically know the potential sample for an online survey, he or she should preface the questionnaire with a full introduction to the purpose and subject matter of the survey as well as instructions for completion procedures.

TRANSITIONAL INSTRUCTIONS

Transitional instructions appear in the questionnaire wherever there are **transitions** from one topic to another. Examples of such instructions appear in Figure 3.1 (preceding Question 2) and Figure 3.3, where the instructions are provided primarily so that the respondent knows the topic of the questions is changing. The questions that preceded this transitional statement asked the respondent about his or her experiences with radial keratotomy; the instruction is included to make it clear to the respondent that the next set of questions will be about a new topic. Such instructions give respondents a chance to "catch their breath" and help them change the focus of their thinking.

The instructions preceding Question 2 in Figure 3.1 are more elaborate. Here, the instructions are not given simply for purposes of transition; rather, they provide a context. Respondents are told that they are going to be asked questions about their experience with corrective lenses. The instructions mention that some respondents have experienced a lot of changes in their lens-wearing patterns since they had surgery, whereas others have experienced little change. The purpose of this statement is to inform respondents that the surveyor expects to find a variety of experiences reported. The respondents are also given a brief instruction about how to answer the questions, namely, "Circle the number that corresponds to your answer."

QUESTION-ANSWERING INSTRUCTIONS

In some cases, surveyors need to provide respondents with relatively elaborate instructions regarding how to fill out questionnaires. These are the third kind of instructions: those whose major purpose is to tell respondents how to go about answering the questions. We needed to include such **question-answering instructions** for the first set of questions in the PERK Study. We asked respondents to read and answer 63 questions that assessed both their vision and their opinions about their vision. The answer categories were the same for all 63 questions and used a 7-point Likert-type scale. The instructions read as follows:

> The first set of questions asks about your overall vision **right now** during the past week. In answering these questions, answer in terms of your **usual** lens-wearing pattern during the past week.
>
> In answering each question, use a range from one (1) to seven (7) where "1" stands for "strongly agree" and "7" stands for "strongly disagree." If you "strongly

agree" with the statement, circle 1; if you agree less strongly, circle 2, which stands for "agree pretty strongly," etc.

For some populations, surveyors would be wise to provide an explicit interpretation of what *each* of the seven numbers in such a scale stands for. In this case, we knew that this sample of respondents had successfully answered similarly formatted questions in the past, so we did not spell out what each number represented. There is a fine line between giving a respondent enough instructions and giving too many. If the surveyor is going to err, however, it is probably better to err on the side of giving too many instructions rather than too few.

Checklist for Writing Instructions

✓ Decide whether general instructions will be given in a cover letter, in the questionnaire, or both.

✓ Tell respondents what the questionnaire is about, what they are being asked to do, and why.

✓ Tell respondents what to do with the completed questionnaire.

✓ Identify places where transition instructions are needed (e.g., change of topic, context for questions that follow).

✓ Determine whether detailed instructions need to be provided for a subset of questions.

Projecting the Surveyor's Ideas Onto Respondents

Surveyors in all substantive areas are concerned with being as objective as possible in how they develop research questions and collect data to test those questions. Because all researchers are human beings, it is probably impossible to eliminate all aspects of **subjectivity** from a research project, but the aim should be to minimize **bias** and subjectivity as much as possible. The various suggestions that we have made regarding how to decide on a research question, write the questions, and create the response categories are all intended to help the surveyor achieve the ultimate goal of maximizing the **objectivity** of the data collected. In collecting data from and about people, one of the most difficult things that surveyors must do is to minimize the extent to which they project their own ideas about how people behave or what they think about onto the survey respondents.

Surveyors must be particularly sensitive to this problem and vigilant when they design mail questionnaires. The *ways* in which questions are asked, the *number* of questions and the *order* in which they are asked, the ranges and types of *response categories* provided, and the *instructions* given all provide surveyors with opportunities for making the data come out the way *they think* the world is organized. If, for example, we are convinced that there are a lot of workplace assaults, and that they occur because there are too many handguns available and because employers provide insufficient security, we can construct a questionnaire that will tend to confirm our perceptions by ignoring many of the recommendations we have made in this chapter.

In the questionnaire we designed to study workplace assaults, we asked only about assaults or threats that happened to the respondent within a specific time period. While we were designing our questionnaire, we conducted focus groups with union members. In the focus groups, most of the members reported that they had not been attacked, but they knew someone who had been attacked, or they knew someone who knew someone else who had been attacked. One of the simplest ways we could have biased the estimates of attacks that we would get would have been to ask respondents about the number of attacks they had heard about rather than restricting our questions to attacks that they themselves experienced. Asking respondents to report on attacks they had heard about undoubtedly would have raised the numbers of attacks reported, but the increase would have been an artificial one, because it is likely that multiple respondents would have heard about the *same* attack. If both Respondent A and Respondent B had told us they knew someone who was attacked and we failed to find out who that person was, when the attack occurred, and so on, we would have been likely to conclude that *two* attacks occurred when, in fact, both respondents might have been reporting the same attack.

Similarly, if we were biased toward thinking that guns are used in most attacks, the answer categories we created for Question 27 in Figure 3.4 might have consisted of just two choices: "gun" and "other." With no other kind of weapon listed, respondents might well have overreported the use of guns, simply because it is easier to circle the number associated with "gun" than it is to fill in the blank associated with "other."

Figure 3.6 shows two of the five questions we actually used in the Workplace Assault Study. If we had had the biases suggested above (and were not vigilant in striving for objectivity in spite of our biases), there are many things we could have done in designing these questions to maximize the chances that the data collected would support our biases. First, we could have restricted our questions to asking about the presence of security personnel only and not bothered to ask Question 31, about security features and devices other than personnel. Second, we could have instructed the respondent to circle only one answer to Question 31. Because "security personnel" is only one of eight security devices listed in the response choices for this question, it is likely that the restriction to a single answer would have resulted in respondents' reporting fewer security personnel. Third, in Question 32, we similarly could have restricted the respondent to one answer, or we could have provided fewer options. For example, we might have provided only Option 1 ("Security personnel are always present in the same place") and Option 5 ("There are no security personnel at my work-site").

31. Which of the following security features/devices are available where you work:

CIRCLE ALL THAT APPLY

Locked doors to outside of building 1

Locked office doors 2

Limited public access to work areas
(counter, locked door, or other barrier) 3

Door alarms 4

Video cameras—monitored 5

Video cameras—unmonitored 6

Electronic key cards 7

Security personnel 8

Other. 9

    Please describe: _____

No security devices. 10

32. To what extent are security personnel present at your worksite:

CIRCLE ALL THAT APPLY

Security personnel are always present in the same place 1
    Please describe where they are located:

_____

Security personnel rove/roam. 2

Security personnel are on call 3

Security personnel monitor alarms and/or video monitors. . . 4

There are no security personnel at my worksite 5

Figure 3.6.   Assessing the Presence of Security Features in the Workplace

In this section, we have demonstrated just a few of the ways in which surveyors can restrict or bias the information they collect about people through the construction of self-administered questionnaires. Improperly designed and poorly tested questionnaires always present a risk. Consequently, surveyors who use questionnaires to collect data must always remain aware of what their own biases are and be vigilant about developing techniques that will keep those biases from creeping into their questionnaires.

Checklist for Minimizing Bias

- ✓ Be aware of your own biases.
- ✓ Develop neutral questions.
- ✓ Ask enough questions to cover the topic adequately.
- ✓ Pay attention to the order of questions.
- ✓ Provide an exhaustive range of response categories.
- ✓ Write clear and unbiased instructions.
- ✓ Take sufficient time to develop the questionnaire.

Pretesting, Pilot Testing, and Revising Questionnaires

The first draft of a questionnaire is never perfect and ready to administer. All questionnaires should be pretested or pilot-tested.

PRETESTING

Surveyors use **pretests** to test sections of questionnaires. In some cases, they conduct pretests of mail questionnaires using interviewers or focus groups. For example, in the Workplace Assault Study, we did our first pretests with focus groups.[1] Union personnel helped us to get three different groups of union members together, and we asked each group to do three things:

- Complete the questionnaire as it existed at that time

- Suggest what other items should be added to the questionnaire

- Discuss aspects of the questionnaire that might be changed

We mentioned earlier that one of the things we learned in the focus groups was that many members had not experienced attacks themselves but knew of others who had; some focus group members even suggested that we should include questions on the questionnaire about threats and attacks that had occurred to persons other than the respondent. Although we did not adopt that suggestion, we did use some of the other suggestions that participants gave us.

We wanted to include questions asking respondents to describe their work locations, but we were somewhat unsure about how many questions we should ask and how we should structure them. Information we gained in the focus groups was particularly helpful to us in our work on that section of the questionnaire. We also became aware of something that we did not act on at that point in the questionnaire development process, but that became particularly salient after we finished our pilot test. Focus group members made us aware that even though many employees did not report actually having been attacked or threatened on the job, they clearly felt vulnerable to such events.

PILOT TESTING

In a **pilot study**, the complete questionnaire is tested using the administrative procedures that will be used in the study. In the Workplace Assault Study, the participants were to be members of two union locals, so for the pilot test we asked each of the locals to provide us with the names and addresses of 10 members. We created a cover letter and had it signed by both a union official and the senior author. The packet that we mailed to each of the 20 potential respondents contained the cover letter, the questionnaire, and a self-addressed, stamped envelope for the respondent to use to return the completed questionnaire to us. Two weeks after we mailed the packets, we sent follow-up postcards to all 20 respondents to remind them that they had been sent the questionnaires. The postcards thanked those who had already returned their questionnaires and asked those who had not to please do so; they also included a phone number that respondents could call if they wanted more information (Figure 3.7 displays the text of the postcard). Two weeks later, or 4 weeks after the original mailing, we sent a second complete mailing to all of the persons in the pilot-test sample from whom we had not received completed questionnaires.

January 24, 1995

About one week ago we sent you a questionnaire about workplace safety. Your name was randomly selected from a Local 660 membership list to participate in this survey.

If you have already returned the questionnaire, please accept our sincere thanks. If not, please do it today. Because it was sent to only a small number of Local 660 members, we very much need your questionnaire if the results are to accurately represent the opinion and experiences of Local 660 members.

If you did not receive the questionnaire, or it got misplaced, please call me at 300-855-5555 and I will get another one in the mail to you immediately.

Sincerely,

Linda Bourque, Ph.D.
UCLA School of Public Health

Figure 3.7.   Example of a Follow-Up Postcard

After all the mailings, we received 12 questionnaires, or 60% of those sent; 6 of them were returned after the first mailing, 3 after the second mailing, and 3 after the third mailing. We considered this a good response rate *until* we realized that 9 of the 12 persons who returned questionnaires were members of one of the two locals. Thus we had a 90% response rate for one local and only a 25% response rate for the other. The question was, why the huge difference? It turned out that it had to do with how union leaders selected persons for the pilot study. The first local selected 20 people randomly, and we then sent questionnaires to 10 of the 20. The second local selected persons for the pilot study because the union leader knew them and knew that they were members of a committee concerned with workplace assault. Needless to say, the individuals in the latter group were more aware of and concerned about workplace assault and, as a result, were more motivated to participate in the study. However, they were not representative of the population of the local. Thus the 25% response rate we achieved with the members of the other local was probably a better indication of what we would get with the questionnaire as it was then designed.

We thought for some time about how we could increase our response rate in the real study. We finally decided that we needed to do a number of different things to increase potential respondents' motivation to answer the questionnaire. The first thing we did was to talk with union leaders in the two locals. Because they were interested in the study and had, in fact, asked us to conduct it, they suggested some changes that we could make in both the questionnaire and the mailings, and they outlined what they could do to publicize the study.

We ended up changing the questionnaire and its administration in five ways. First, the union leaders suggested that we publish a brief article about the survey in the monthly newsletter of one of the locals, timing it to appear in the issue that immediately preceded the **mailing** of the questionnaire. We also developed a flyer that was sent to union stewards and others to put on bulletin boards at the various work sites. Second, with the union's help, we mailed an advance letter to each of the 1,744 persons constituting our sample approximately 2 weeks before we sent the questionnaire itself (see Figure 3.8). This letter was on union **letter-**

head and was signed by union leaders. The purpose of both activities was to raise awareness within the target population and encourage all members of the sample to participate.

SOCIAL SERVICES
UNION

AMERICAN
FEDERATION
OF NURSES

309 SO. RAYMOND
AVENUE
PASADENA
CALIFORNIA
91105
818-796-0051
FAX 818-796-2335

January 5, 1995

Dear Member,

    You have been randomly selected from our membership list of Los Angeles County employees to take part in a survey about personal safety at the workplace. Your participation in the survey is very important. When you receive the questionnaire in the mail from UCLA, please fill it out and return it as soon as possible.

    Our members who work for Los Angeles County are concerned about personal safety on the job. The union has raised this issue with management in contract negotiations and by filing grievances, but with only limited success. We need to do more. The SEIU Health & Safety Department and the Injury Prevention Research Center at UCLA's School of Public Health have worked with Local 535 members to develop a questionnaire addressing these issues. The questionnaire asks about concerns regarding personal safety at work as well experiences involving fear, verbal abuse, threats, and assaults on the job. Employers will not reveal this type of information. **It has to come from you!**

    The results of this study will document the extent and nature of risks that our members encounter at work. Hopefully, future projects will address policies and practices intended to improve personal safety of Local 535's Los Angeles County workers.

    Please fill out the survey from UCLA as soon as you receive it in the mail! If you have any questions or concerns about the survey, please feel free to call Wilma Cadorna at Local 535 or Deborah Riopelle, M.S.P.H. at UCLA at 310-825-4053.

Thanks for your help.

Sincerely,

Jerry L. Clyde
President, Social Services Chapter
SEIU Local 535

Linda Bourque, Ph.D.
UCLA School of Public Health

Figure 3.8.   Example of an Advance Letter

Third, again at the union's suggestion, we decided that the original cover letter was too imposing and that we needed to do three things to make the questionnaire packet more user-friendly. First, we downplayed the topic of violence and assault in the cover letter and emphasized personal safety at work. We also made this adjustment in emphasis in the questionnaire itself, changing the title of the questionnaire from "Physical Assault in the Workplace" to "Personal Safety at Work." Second, we shortened the entire cover letter itself as well as the sentences within it and simplified the language (Figures 3.9 and 3.10 display the original and redesigned cover letters). Finally, we added a flyer to the packet of materials. The flyer was designed to be eye-catching and to give potential respondents some basic information that we hoped would increase their interest in reading the cover letter and completing the questionnaire (see Figure 3.11).

We also made two changes in the questionnaire itself. First, as noted above, we de-emphasized violence and assault and emphasized workplace safety. We did this by changing the title, modifying the wording of some questions, and changing the order of some questions. Originally, the questionnaire was divided into four parts presented in the following order: questions about physical assaults experienced in the past year, questions about threats experienced in the past month, questions about the workplace, and demographic questions about the respondent. We decided that this order was problematic for two reasons. First, by starting with questions about assault and threat, the questionnaire emphasized violence and assault. Our pretest suggested that this topic might be too extreme for our respondents and needed to be introduced less abruptly and more gradually. Second, we realized that the majority of respondents would *not* have experienced any assaults or threats, and so would be instructed to skip through the first half or two-thirds of the questionnaire. In contrast, everyone in our sample had a work site to describe and, remembering back to our pretests with the focus groups, we knew that some *felt* threatened in

SOCIAL SERVICES
UNION

AMERICAN
FEDERATION
OF NURSES

309 So. RAYMOND
AVENUE
PASADENA
CALIFORNIA
91105
818-796-0051
FAX 818-796-2335

October 7, 1994

Dear Member,

    We need your help to stop workplace violence. Many people
are worried that workplace violence has increased dramatically
over the past several years. Studies have shown that homicide
ranks as one of the leading causes of work-related injury deaths.
However, little is really known about assaults and threats of
violence in the workplace. The Service Employees International
Union, AFL-CIO (Locals 660 and 535) is concerned about the
violence its members may encounter on a day-to-day basis.
Therefore, in cooperation with the Southern California Injury
Prevention Research Center at the UCLA School of Public Health,
SEIU is conducting a study of workplace violence. Results from
this survey will help determine the extent and nature of threats
and assaults that occur in the workplace and security measures
which are already in place or which may be needed.

    We need your help. Enclosed is a copy of the questionnaire
that will be used in the study. This version of the questionnaire
includes questions about:

    *   Your experience with workplace threats and assaults
    *   Security measures at your work site
    *   The type of work you do and the place where you work
    *   Your opinion about the content and format of the
         questionnaire

    Based on your comments and suggestions, the questionnaire
will be revised before a final copy is mailed out to other members
of Locals 660 and 535 in Los Angeles County. Please take the time
to complete the questionnaire and return it in the enclosed self-
addressed stamped envelope. It would be very helpful to have your
completed questionnaire returned to us by October 24, 1994. We
would like to send out the final survey as soon as possible.

    Your responses are confidential. No names or individual
information will be used or released to your employer. If you
have any questions or concerns, please feel free to call Deborah
Riopelle, M.S.P.H. at UCLA, (310) 825-4053 or Wilma Cadorna at
Local 535 (818) 796-0051.

Sincerely,

David Bullock   Linda Bourque Ph.D.
Southern Regional Director   UCLA School of Public Health

Figure 3.9.   Example of an Original Cover Letter

**Social Services
Union**

**American
Federation
of Nurses**

309 So. Raymond
Avenue
Pasadena
California
91105
818-796-0051
Fax 818-796-2335

January 17, 1995

Dear Member,

We need your help to improve personal safety on the job for Los Angeles County employees. Little is really known about personal safety and security while at work. The Service Employees International Union, Local 535 is concerned about the risks its members may encounter on a day-to-day basis. In cooperation with the Southern California Injury Prevention Research Center (SCIPRC) at the UCLA School of Public Health, we are conducting a study of workplace safety. Results from this survey will help determine measures that could be taken to protect our members.

You have been randomly selected from the membership list of Local 535's Los Angeles County employees to participate in this survey. Only a small proportion of Los Angeles County employees has been selected to participate, so your experiences and thoughts on the subject are very important. You will be representing many employees who are similar to yourself.

Enclosed is a copy of the questionnaire that includes questions about:

* **The type of work you do and the place where you work**
* **Personal safety measures at your work site**
* **How safe or unsafe you feel at work**
* **Your experience with workplace threats and assaults**

Please take the time to complete the questionnaire and return it in the enclosed self-addressed stamped envelope. It would be very helpful to have your completed questionnaire returned to us by **January 25, 1995.**

Your responses are confidential. No names or individual information will be used or released to your employer. If you have any questions or concerns, please feel free to call Deborah Riopelle, M.S.P.H. at UCLA, (310) 825-4053 or Wilma Cadorna at Local 535.

Sincerely,

Jerry L. Clyde
President, Social Services Chapter
SEIU Local 535

Linda Bourque, Ph.D.
UCLA School of Public Health

Figure 3.10. Example of a Final Cover Letter

HOW SAFE IS YOUR WORKPLACE?

DO YOU FEEL UNSAFE OR INSECURE AT WORK?

HAVE YOU OR ANY OF YOUR CO-WORKERS EVER BEEN THE VICTIM OF THREATS, ASSAULTS, OR VIOLENCE ON THE JOB?

LOCAL 660
IS WORKING TO CURB WORKPLACE VIOLENCE.

WE NEED YOUR HELP!

PLEASE TAKE A FEW MOMENTS TO COMPLETE THE ENCLOSED CONFIDENTIAL SURVEY.

WORKING TOGETHER, WE CAN MAKE OUR WORKPLACE SAFER.

Figure 3.11. Example of a Flyer Used for Motivation

their work sites even if they had not been assaulted or threatened. Thus there was a perception of threat even if there was no objective evidence of it.

These two reasons in combination led us to reorder the questionnaire. We first asked respondents to describe their work sites and the security of their work sites. We then asked about threats they had experienced, followed by questions on assaults experienced and ending with the demographic questions. The changes did appear to increase our response rate somewhat. Of the original 1,744 questionnaires mailed, 38 had incorrect addresses and were returned to us. Of the remaining 1,706, 310, or 18%, were completed and returned after the first mailing. Another 258, or 15%, were completed and returned in response to the postcard. Thus before we sent out the second complete packet, 568 respondents, or 33% of our sample, had returned completed questionnaires. Another 285 completed questionnaires were returned in response to the second mailing of the complete packet, bringing our total response rate after three mailings to 50%. We considered this insufficient for our purposes, so we turned to telephone follow-up; attempts were made to conduct telephone interviews with all of the remaining 853 union members who had not responded to any of the three mailings.

VALUE OF PRETESTS AND PILOT TESTS

We conducted both a pretest and a pilot test in the Workplace Assault Study. Both provided us with valuable information, and both convinced us to change aspects of the questionnaire and the administrative procedures. They also made us aware of some biases that both we and the union leaders had about the topic of the study and this population of workers. We had assumed that union members would be highly motivated to answer questions about assault in the workplace and that, in their eagerness to answer such questions, they would not be threatened by the topic. In fact, two things appeared to be going on. Although some proportion of these union members were concerned about workplace safety, when the questionnaire began by asking respondents to describe actual assaults, most had none to describe, and thus their motivation to answer the questions decreased. By changing the order of the questionnaire and increasing publicity about the study, we were able to overcome some of this resistance.

Surveyors can evaluate many things by conducting pretests and pilot tests. They can learn how well their questions or instructions are understood and how comprehensive their response categories are. They may learn that they need to change the sequence of questions or modify their planned administrative procedures. Sometimes a surveyor needs to ascertain how well a translated version of a questionnaire works. Pilot tests can also help a surveyor estimate how much the data collection will cost in time and money. In the Workplace Assault Study, the pilot test made us realize that we had underestimated our mailing costs and the amount of personnel time it would take to set up four mailings (an advance letter, an original questionnaire mailing, a follow-up postcard, and a second questionnaire mailing).

Surveyors should always conduct pretests and pilot tests prior to actual data collection, evaluate the results carefully, and apply what they learn in making changes to the questionnaire and the study design. When a surveyor identifies serious or multiple problems during a pretest or pilot test, he or she should make revisions as needed and continue with pretesting until he or she is confident that the data collection instrument is effectively and efficiently obtaining the data needed to test the research question validly and reliably. Respondents for pretests and pilot test should always be representative members of the survey's target population.

Checklist for Conducting Pretests and Pilot Tests

✓ Decide whether pretests, pilot tests, or both are needed.

✓ Decide whether multiple pretests or pilot tests will be needed.

✓ Decide how pretests will be conducted—in focus groups, by interview, in group administrations, or through the mail?

✓ Decide what the sample is for the pilot test or pretest—should it be representative?

✓ Pay careful attention to the results of pretests and pilot tests:

- Do the respondents understand the questions?

- Are instructions clear?

- Is the order of questions appropriate?

- Do both surveyors and respondents clearly understand the objectives of the study?

- Have costs been projected accurately?

Note

1. The use of focus groups to develop questions, item series, and/or concept areas has been increasing in recent years. A focus group usually consists of 8 to 10 participants who are guided by a trained moderator. The moderator is skilled in focus group techniques and either has some background in the topic under study or is briefed extensively on the topic. The participants are usually recruited at random from the community or may have responded to a survey in the past. If the topic area is one requiring particular knowledge or skills, recruiting is directed exclusively toward individuals with those skills. A focus group session typically lasts 90 minutes, is led by the moderator using a guide of topic areas, and consists of an open discussion about the subject area. The discussion is usually audio- or videotaped, and sometimes transcribed. Surveyors use what they learn through focus groups to develop questions for surveys. In the case of the Workplace Assault Study, the focus groups were designed to test an existing questionnaire using cognitive questionnaire development techniques, which determine what respondents hear when asked a question and what they think the question is asking. In a focus group, the surveyor or moderator has the opportunity to determine how each individual processes a question in a situation that closely resembles a one-on-one interview.

4 Format of the Questionnaire

Neophyte surveyors make two common errors in developing and **formatting** questionnaires: They indicate in instructions or cover letters that the questionnaire will "only take 5 minutes to fill out," and they format the questionnaire to make it look as short as possible. Often, an unsophisticated surveyor will attempt to make an entire questionnaire fit on two sides of one page. The surveyors' stated objective in both cases is "to increase response rates." Both are errors, however; in fact, they may *reduce* response rates for a number of reasons. If a research question is worth studying, collecting the necessary data from an individual to shed light on that question can rarely be accomplished in less than 5 minutes, regardless of how the data are collected. It takes a potential respondent 5 minutes just to open the envelope and read the cover letter or introduction to a mail questionnaire. In the case of online surveys, there is no accurate way for surveyors to judge how long a questionnaire will take to download to an individual's personal computer. Much depends on the volume of Internet traffic at the moment, the caliber of the hardware and software the recipient is using, and the complexity of the questionnaire design itself.

When you have gone to all the trouble to develop a questionnaire, print it, and mail it, you want to be certain that all that work results in the collection of sufficient information to answer your research question. This is no less true for online surveys, which require careful planning, formatting, and programming. We know people who have eliminated demographic questions from questionnaires because they wanted "to save space," only to discover during data analysis that without demographic information on their respondents they were unable to answer certain important questions about their sample population.

Length

Some novice surveyors squish all of their questions onto two sides of one sheet of paper for the same reason: They want to make the questionnaire look shorter. In doing this, however, they usually eliminate questions that would have gathered important information from their study, *or* they make the questionnaire unreadable. There are no spaces between questions, and margins are small or nonexistent. The respondent needs a magnifying glass to read the tiny print and has trouble finding or differentiating between response categories.

In formatting a questionnaire, you want to "help" the respondent move through it. One of the most valuable things you can do to help the respondent is to leave sufficient space between questions, between each question and its set of response categories, and between the alternative response categories. Space is as important as content in the presentation of a questionnaire. It has been suggested that mail questionnaires should be no longer than 12 pages; in general, most range between 4 and 12 pages. However, longer questionnaires can be used under two circumstances: when the respondents are highly motivated and when the reason for the additional number of pages is largely a function of increasing the questionnaire's readability.

Vertical Format

Notice that in the PERK Study and the Workplace Assault Study (see Figures 3.1 through 3.4 and 3.6 in Chapter 3), we used a **vertical format** for our questions and answer categories. There are other methods for maximizing the clarity and order of a questionnaire as well, such as the use of shading, boxes, and arrows; a questionnaire may also be set up in a newspaper column format. The 1990 U.S. Census form provides an example of a mail questionnaire that uses boxes and a newspaper column format to clarify how the respondent should proceed through the questions (see Figure 2.1 in Chapter 2).

We like a vertical format for two reasons. First, it simultaneously differentiates the question from the possible response categories and differentiates the response categories from each other. If, for example, we had used a horizontal format for Question 4 in Figure 3.2, we might have ended up with something like this:

> In general, would you say your health is:
> Excellent 1
> Very Good 2
> Good 3
> Fair, or 4
> Poor 5

or even this:

> In general, would you say your health is:
> ____Excellent
> ____Very Good
> ____Good
> ____Fair, or
> ____Poor

Many surveyors think that respondents are unable to work with precoded questions such as those used in our examples. Instead, they have respondents put check marks next to appropriate answer categories. Then, for reasons we have never been able to explain, they put the spaces for the check marks *in front of* the answer categories, *and,* to save space, they use a horizontal format! What's wrong with this strategy?

First of all, we in the United States are used to filling out precoded questionnaires. We have no difficulty circling a number, clicking a mouse, or filling in a box on a scannable data form. Second, we read from left to right in English. Putting answer spaces to the *left* of the words or phrases to which they correspond is counterintuitive. Third, horizontal formatting of answer categories increases the likelihood that respondents will make errors. In the second example above, a respondent might easily confuse the alternatives and put a check mark in the blank before "Good," which corresponds to an answer of "Good," when what the respondent *really* intends to say is that his or her health is "Very Good." Similarly in the first example, even with the precoding and the dots linking each response with its numeric code, a respondent may well select the number physically *closest* to the answer he or she means to give rather than the code linked to it by dots.

Finally, a vertical format in which codes are already assigned and placed to the right of the response categories makes data entry much easier and leads to fewer errors. With most answers placed to the right of each page, the person doing data entry can simply follow the codes down the side of the page when entering the data.

The one exception to vertical format in our examples is shown in Questions 12 and 13 in Figure 3.1 (Chapter 3). For these stem questions, instead of simply asking respondents to circle the numbers that correspond to the situations for which they use reading glasses, we ask them to select either "yes" or "no." We used this format in this case because the information gathered by these questions was particularly important in the PERK Study, and we knew that the inclusion of the yes/no column would tend to increase the likelihood that the respondent would read each activity. Similarly, a horizontal format is useful when the respondent is going to be using the same answer categories for an entire set of questions—for example, on a Likert-type scale. Figure 4.1 provides an example.

Grids

Both Figure 3.1 and Figure 4.1 provide simple examples of **grids.** Using a grid format can enable a surveyor to save space on a questionnaire, for example, when a series of questions to be asked will use the same selection of answer categories. Grids are particularly popular with surveyors who are writing series of questions to be used in developing scales or indexes. They can also be used to format multiple sets of question sequences. Such grids are usually rather complex and, as such, are difficult for a respondent to work through in a self-administered questionnaire. Thus they are usually used only in interviewer-administered questionnaires.

Spacing

Notice that in all of our examples we have left substantial space between questions and response categories and have used dots to indicate clearly which numeric code is associated with which answer. In these examples, we have used at least double spacing between questions and between each question and its response categories. Within each set of answer categories, we have used 1.5 spacing. Notice also that we have indented the sets of answers under the questions to help clarify where one question stops and the next begins. Where we have dependent questions—for example, 1A and 1B in Figure 3.2—these questions are similarly indented. This helps the respondent follow the skip instructions that corre-

1. The first set of questions asks about your overall vision **right now** during the past week. In answering these questions, answer in terms of your **usual** lens-wearing pattern during the past week.

In answering each question, use a range from one (1) to seven (7), where "1" stands for "strongly agree" and "7" stands for "strongly disagree." If you "strongly agree" with the statement, circle the "1"; if you agree less strongly, circle the "2," which stands for "agree pretty strongly," etc.

			Strongly Agree			Neutral			Strongly Disagree
V20	1)	I can see well far away **without** correction	1	2	3	4	5	6	7
V21	2)	When I drive at night, I have a lot of problems with glare from lights	1	2	3	4	5	6	7
V22	3)	If I drive in the morning I have to wear my lenses, but if I drive in the late afternoon (before dusk) I can drive without my lenses	1	2	3	4	5	6	7
V23	4)	I have a lot of trouble with glare in my operated eye(s)	1	2	3	4	5	6	7
V24	5)	When I read, I need more light than I used to	1	2	3	4	5	6	7
V25	6)	I hate wearing reading glasses	1	2	3	4	5	6	7
V26	7)	Without my lenses, I use one eye to look at things that are close to me and the other eye to look at things that are far away	1	2	3	4	5	6	7
V27	8)	Even with my usual lenses (if worn), my visual acuity is not as good at night as it is during the day	1	2	3	4	5	6	7

Figure 4.1.   Example of a Likert-Type Scale With Variable Names

spond to the answer given to Question 1. Respondents who say yes are asked to answer Questions 1A and 1B, whereas those who say no are asked to go on to Question 2. The combination of indentation, spacing, and instructions that are set off from the rest of the text—in this case, by capital letters—helps the respondent move expeditiously through the questionnaire.

Printing the questionnaire as a booklet (that is, folding the pages in the middle lengthwise and stapling them at the fold to form a "book") is a format we particularly like to use when funds are available to do it. Questionnaires that are printed this way look more professional than other kinds of questionnaires. When using the booklet format, we generally use 8 1/2-by-17-inch paper, because this allows us to use larger print.

Often, surveyors produce the pages of questionnaires on word processors, and the page size is then reduced during printing and production of the booklets. In the process, however, the print is also reduced. Small print or ornate print can be difficult for some respondents to read, especially those over age 50 who need to wear reading glasses or who have difficulty seeing in poor light. We recommend using a 12-point pitch size and an easily read **font** with equal character spacing, such as Courier. Surveyors should avoid using italics, which are difficult to read, and fonts that use proportional spacing (i.e., the letter *m* takes up more space than the letter *i*), as they can cause alignment problems (and extreme headaches) in the setup of a questionnaire.

Print and Paper

There should be good contrast between the printed words and the paper on which the questionnaire is printed. We recommend that, when in doubt, surveyors use black print on a white background. Some colors of paper, such as the currently fashionable neon colors, are difficult for respondents to look at for long periods of time. Also, surveyors should avoid using colors that lower the contrast for color-blind persons. There is one situation where printing questionnaires on different colors of paper can be very helpful, however. If there are different forms of the questionnaire for different respondents (say, males and females), the surveyor may want to print them on different colors of paper (the questionnaire for females on white paper and the questionnaire for males on pale blue paper, for example). Then the surveyor will be able to look at a pile of questionnaires and know immediately which form of the questionnaire should be given to a particular respondent; this technique reduces the risk that any respondent will receive the wrong form of the questionnaire.

As our examples show, we use combinations of **boldface type**, <u>underlining</u>, and CAPITALS when we want to emphasize something in the text of a question or give instructions about how to fill out the questionnaire. We consistently use all capital letters in providing instructions—for example, the instructions "CIRCLE ALL THAT APPLY," "GO TO Q2," and "ANSWER A." We use boldface and sometimes underlining to emphasize key words or phrases in a question—for example, in Question 9 in Figure 3.1, "Did anyone in the PERK Study ever tell you that **after** you had surgery you might have to wear glasses or other lenses for **reading** and other **close work**?"

Surveyors also use other techniques, such as shading or boxing information. As we noted earlier, we do not recommend the use of italics because we have found that italicized text is difficult for respondents to read, but other surveyors do use italics for emphasis or in instructions. We also discourage the use of shading in questionnaires because it reduces the contrast between the print and the background, and so makes it more difficult for the respondent to see and read the questions or instructions. We also do not recommend putting too much information in bold type. Some surveyors print all of their instructions in bold, but we have found that if a page contains a lot of instructions in bold, the text of the questions themselves and the response categories can tend to get lost, with the result that the respondent sees the instructions very well but misses key phrases in the questions or key answer alternatives.

Consistency

Whatever the size and format of print you select for the questionnaire, the key is to be consistent. If you decide that instructions contained within the body of the questionnaire are going to be underlined, then you should make sure that *all* the instructions in the body of the questionnaire are underlined and that underlining is *not* used to indicate emphasis in the text of questions. Instead, use boldface type for emphasis.

You should also be consistent in the spacing you insert between questions and in the use of indentations. If you decide to use single spacing within the text of individual questions and double spacing between questions, then be sure that you do so throughout the questionnaire. Notice that our examples are consistent in the way the answer categories are lined up. In Figure 3.1 (Chapter 3), the text of all the questions is aligned on the same indent, and the answer categories for all questions are similarly aligned on a further indent, with the beginnings of all the answers lined up and the respective codes lined up.

Splitting Questions Between Pages

A common error that new surveyors often make is to split a question between pages, either separating the instructions for a section from the questions that it is describing or separating related and dependent questions across pages. Sometimes this occurs because the surveyor is trying to save space, but often it happens simply because the surveyor doesn't think. Take a moment to look at Figure 3.1 in Chapter 3. Imagine that there was sufficient space on a prior page for the instructions that precede Question 2 but insufficient space for the question itself. Some surveyors would go ahead and put the instructions on the prior page and then wonder why respondents subsequently have difficulty understanding the questions that follow on the next page.

Another common error is to break up related questions. For example, a surveyor might place the instructions and Question 2 on one page because there is sufficient room, but then place Question 2A on a subsequent page. Because Question 2A is logically dependent on Question 2, this practice increases the probability that respondents never see Question 2A or that they do not understand it.

Finally, look at Question 12 in Figure 3.1. Here, both of the two parts of the question are followed by long lists of possible responses. Yet another common error is to split such a list of possible responses between two pages (again, surveyors most commonly do this to save space). When such a list is split up, respondents often fail to see the complete list and, as a result, never read or consider the responses that appear on the second page. Splitting up a list of response choices is particularly problematic when respondents are asked to select a *single* response to the question. Because respondents do not weigh the possible answers on the second page equally with those they see on the first page, they select responses on the second page significantly less often.

Occasionally, a list of response choices is too long to be printed on a single page even if the question (e.g., Question 12) starts at the top of the page. In general, we recommend against using such long lists in a mail questionnaire. However, sometimes it is unavoidable. If a list must continue onto a second page, the questionnaire *must* be printed in booklet form, with the question itself and the first part of the list of responses on a left-hand (i.e., even-numbered) page and the continuation of the list on the facing right-hand page.

Formatting Online Questionnaires

Those of us who routinely work in survey research know that, as a group, we have a strong tendency to adopt new technologies as soon as they become available and to try to push the uses of new technologies to the maximum. The opportunities that computerization has offered to survey research have led many a researcher into the trap of making the collection of data more complicated than it needs to be. Their study expenses escalate, and the resulting data often contain more errors than they would have if the surveyors had kept their instruments and their methods more straight-forward. Online questionnaires, just like paper-and-pencil questionnaires, need to be user-friendly.

LENGTH

It is just as important to keep online questionnaires to a reasonable length as it is to limit the length of mail question-naires. We mentioned that mail questionnaires should be no longer than 12 pages; in general, the same is true for ques-tionnaires administered online. As is the case with mail sur-veys, surveyors can use longer questionnaires online when the respondents are highly motivated. To date, no research has compared paper-and-pencil questionnaires and online questionnaires in terms of respondents' reading speed and comprehension. Many personal computer users find it diffi-cult to read lengthy text documents on their computer screens. Instead, they print out hard copies of such docu-ments, so they can read them more carefully or at their leisure. Most of the Web-administered surveys we have seen have stated at the outset the length of time it typically takes to complete the questionnaire; usually, the estimated time is between 15 and 25 minutes.

By their nature, online questionnaires automatically move the respondent through the questions. Although sur-veyors designing online questionnaires need not be concerned about spacing between the questions, they do need to keep each question and all of its answer alternatives on one screen. Just as in paper questionnaires, when surveyors try to fit more onto a screen by using a smaller font size or by letting the text go from margin to margin, they only make it harder for the respondent to read; in addition, such design choices may result in the questionnaire's taking longer to download. If the words on the screen are too small or too crammed together to be read easily, the respondent may grow frustrated and, as a result, terminate the interview. Many online surveys incorporate a progress indicator, which looks much like a temperature gauge, on each screen to show the respondent how much of the questionnaire he or she has completed and how much remains to be done.

FORMAT

As mentioned above, a surveyor creating an online questionnaire should make sure that each question and its response options appear together on one screen. Asking the respondent to go back and forth between screens is akin to breaking a question across two pages of a paper questionnaire. Respondents should not be expected to go back to prior screens or pages to reread questions. Furthermore, the software used to design online questionnaires often will not allow respondents to go back to prior pages or screens; if they do, they may risk breaking the connection, or they may affect the program operation in some other way.

Software programs make possible the inclusion of a wide variety of pictures and other graphic elements in online surveys; surveyors should give careful consideration to how they use such elements. Grids are easily employed in online questionnaires, but of course the surveyor must be careful not to exceed the numbers of columns and rows that fit comfortably on a screen. Surveyors designing online questionnaires can also employ multiple colors on the screen and incorporate shading, highlighting, and pictures in their survey instruments. However, although such features may seem like good tools for focusing respondents' attention on the questions, they may not accomplish that goal at all. What the questionnaire designer sees on his or her monitor may not be what every respondent sees. Graphics do not transfer to all operating systems equally, and surveyors cannot assume that all potential respondents will have systems that are compatible with their own graphics software.

Like paper questionnaires, online questionnaires should be as consistent in presentation as possible. When a questionnaire features new colors, new effects, or other new design elements from screen to screen, it is likely only to confuse the respondent. For the respondent, filling out a questionnaire, in any format, is a learning process. As the respondent goes through the questions, he or she "learns" what it is the surveyor wants, how to read each question and how to answer it. If the questionnaire switches styles often, the respondent is forced not only to "learn" each new format but to "unlearn" the prior format.

To date, very little research has systematically examined how different colors, different formats, and the use of pictures in online questionnaires influence response rates or the validity of responses. The little research that does exist suggests that these features influence both response rates and the answers that respondents select as "their answers."

Checklist for Formatting Questionnaires

✓ Do not give unrealistic time estimates.

✓ Ask enough questions to obtain the information needed.

✓ Use space between questions.

✓ Use vertical format, space, boxes, arrows, shading, or other devices consistently to maximize the clarity and order of questions.

✓ Do not avoid precoded response categories, but clearly indicate the code that corresponds to each response.

✓ Consider the use of simple grids.

✓ Use a booklet format when possible.

✓ Make sure there is good contrast between the print and the paper.

✓ Use 12-point pitch.

✓ Use an easily read, equally spaced font, such as Courier.

✓ Avoid the use of italics.

✓ Use **bold**, <u>underlining</u>, and CAPITALS judiciously and consistently for emphasis and instructions.

✓ Do not split instructions, questions, and associated responses between pages.

Coordinating With Data Entry Personnel and Data Processors

As the questionnaire is being developed, the surveyor needs to consider the needs of the persons who will be doing the data entry and data processing. We have already recommended the **precoding** of closed-ended questions with clear indications of where and how answers are to be recorded. We also recommend that the surveyor set up the protocol by which the data will be entered into the computer before the questionnaire is actually finalized and then provide variable names on the questionnaire itself at the time it is printed. (Given the large variety of data entry programs now available, column information generally is not needed, and putting it on the questionnaire is a waste of time and ink.)

Figure 4.1 provides an example of a set of questions for which the data entry program was preset and the variable names that corresponded to each question in the data set were included on the questionnaire when it was printed. Some survey researchers object to having such information appear on questionnaires that are given to respondents because they believe that respondents do not understand the information and are likely to be confused by it. In our own research, we have not noticed that such information reduces response rates or confuses respondents. Regardless of whether or not surveyors include such information on their questionnaires, they must, at minimum, ensure that the data being collected can be efficiently converted into **machine-readable** form.

The precoding used on paper-and-pencil questionnaires is not relevant for online surveys. Although the answer categories in an online questionnaire are coded before the survey is conducted, the **coding** scheme is transparent to the respondents. As we noted previously, respondents in online surveys mark their responses by using a mouse to click on "radio buttons" or click boxes, or by typing their answers into text boxes. The advantage of an online questionnaire over a paper-and-pencil questionnaire in terms of data entry is that the data are "cleaner"—that is, if the questionnaire is properly programmed, a respondent cannot provide more than one answer to a question when only one answer is desired, nor can he or she enter an answer that is "out of range" (i.e., that does not fit into the numeric codes associated with the available answer categories).

Ending the Questionnaire

The surveyor should end the questionnaire by inviting the respondent to comment on its content, to make suggestions about what the surveyor might have missed, and even to complain about the questionnaire itself. Such questions are often referred to as "ventilation" questions, because they allow respondents to ventilate their feelings about the topic or the questionnaire.

Following any ventilation questions, respondents should be given instructions for mailing back or otherwise returning the questionnaire. Even when the surveyor provides respondents with preaddressed, stamped envelopes to use in returning the questionnaires, these often get lost or mislaid. When that happens, a respondent has no way of knowing how to return the questionnaire unless an address is provided on the questionnaire itself. Letting respondents return completed questionnaires by fax is an option that surveyors might consider.

Finally, the questionnaire should end with a message thanking the respondent for his or her time and cooperation. This is a courtesy due any study participant.

Camera-Ready Copy

If the surveyor has considered all of the points discussed above and resolved any problems with the questionnaire design, and if the content of the questionnaire has been carefully proofread and all errors found have been corrected, the questionnaire is "camera ready," or ready for duplication and production. Usually, questionnaires are either photocopied or set up for offset printing. We discuss these procedures and what they cost in detail in Chapter 5.

Checklist for Finalizing the Questionnaire

✓ Format the questionnaire to facilitate data entry.

✓ Afford respondents the opportunity to comment on the questionnaire.

✓ Make sure the return address is printed on a mail questionnaire.

✓ End the questionnaire with a message thanking the respondent.

✓ Carefully proofread the questionnaire one final time and make any necessary corrections.

✓ Duplicate or print the questionnaire.

Correspondence and the Motivation of Respondents

Every self-administered questionnaire must be accompanied by an explanation of the purposes and **sponsorship** of the study. When questionnaires are distributed to respondents at a single site or on a one-to-one basis, some of this explanation may be provided verbally, with a detailed explanation appearing on the first page of the questionnaire itself. We provided an example of such an explanation in Figure 3.5, which shows the general instructions used on a questionnaire in the PERK Study. Because that questionnaire represented a 10-year follow-up to a study in which respondents had been contacted repeatedly, we did not repeat information about sponsorship in the introductory statement. However, most questionnaires represent the first contact with a respondent and are *not* distributed as part of a multiyear follow-up. Surveyors should always reconfirm, elaborate on, or repeat information in writing, even when some of the information is provided verbally.

A mail questionnaire must *always* be accompanied by a cover letter. Respondent compliance can be increased by a well-written cover letter that explains the purpose of the study, tells how and why the individual was selected to be a respondent, and cites meaningful reasons the individual should participate. The cover letter should stress how important it is for the individual to respond and how important that person is to the research. It is also beneficial for the cover letter to be signed or endorsed by someone with positive name recognition for the respondents. For example, if the sample is composed of individuals who belong to a particular professional organization, it may be helpful for the president of the organization to endorse the study unless, of course, the members of the organization are likely to distrust the leadership.

Obviously, online questionnaires are not accompanied by cover letters, but they do need introductions. Generally, we assume that potential respondents for an online survey did not simply stumble onto the survey Web site, but had some prior information that led them to it. Depending on the sample source, they may have received invitations to participate via an e-mail list to which they belong, or they may have been sent advance letters because the investigator has a list of the names and addresses of individuals he or she wants to respond. Perhaps they saw an invitation to participate on another Web site they visited, or perhaps they were recruited through in-person or telephone contact. Regardless of how they were recruited, respondents for online surveys should always be provided with the same kinds of information that should be given to the respondents in a mailed survey.

Surveyors should include or at least consider including the following 14 elements in any correspondence intended to motivate respondents:

1. Use of letterhead

2. Information about sponsorship

3. Dates

4. Salutation

5. Information on the purpose of the study

6. Reasons an individual's participation is important

7. Information on incentives being offered to encourage respondent participation

8. Use of advance letters

9. Information on how material incentives will be provided or distributed

10. Realistic estimate of the time required to complete the questionnaire

11. Information on how and why the respondent was chosen

12. Explanation of confidentiality and how the data will be handled

13. Provision of a name and phone number to call for information

14. Information on when and how the respondent should return the questionnaire

Figures 3.8 through 3.11 (Chapter 3) provide examples of an advance letter, an original cover letter, a modified cover letter, and a motivational flyer that we used in the Workplace Assault Study.

USE OF LETTERHEAD

The quality of the presentation of all survey materials plays an important part in stimulating respondent interest. Every item sent to respondents should be as attractive and professional looking as possible. Earlier, we described how different colors of paper, style of print, and format of the questionnaire can affect response rates. In Chapter 5, we discuss the relative advantages of hand-addressing envelopes versus typing them and the use of stamps versus metered mail. Although most of these treatments seem to have little effect on response rates, the numbers of returns do increase slightly with the use of special materials.

All surveyors advocate the use of professional letterhead for advance letters and cover letters because it helps establish the importance of the study, gives information about study sponsorship, and serves indirectly as a means of personalizing the contact with the respondent. Being contacted by a recognized, reputable organization serves to legitimate the importance of the study in the respondent's mind, and also emphasizes for the respondent the uniqueness of his or her position as a source of information. All of the advance and cover letters we used in the Workplace Assault Study were printed on the letterheads of the locals of the Service Employees International Union (SEIU) that took part in the study. The examples that appear in Figures 3.8 through 3.10 were all printed on Local 535's letterhead; identical letters that we sent to members of Local 660 were printed on that local's letterhead. We used the SEIU letterhead because it identified the study as a union-sponsored activity and helped establish the survey's legitimacy.

INFORMATION ABOUT SPONSORSHIP

Survey materials sent to respondents should state specifically who is conducting and/or sponsoring the study, as the examples in Figures 3.8 through 3.10 illustrate. Because the Workplace Assault Study was a joint activity of SEIU Locals 535 and 660 and the Southern California Injury Prevention Research Center (SCIPRC) located in the School of Public Health at the University of California, Los Angeles, we mentioned the sponsorship of *both* groups, and representatives of both groups signed both letters. Note that mailings to Local 535 members were signed by the president of the Social Services Chapter of SEIU Local 535, and that mailings to Local 660 members were signed by the general manager of Local 660. All letters were also signed by the senior author as a representative of the SCIPRC at UCLA's School of Public Health.

DATES

It is impossible to overstate the importance of including accurate dates on questionnaire cover letters and other mailings to respondents. Many surveyors simply neglect to put dates on letters, but others do not fully think out the sequence of administrative procedures (see Chapter 5), and, as a consequence, the dates that appear on their cover letters, advance letters, and follow-up materials differ substantially from the actual dates of the mailings. The dates on all materials sent to respondents should be either the same as the postmark dates on the envelopes or a day or two preceding those dates.

SALUTATION

The salutations used on advance letters, cover letters, and questionnaires can make a difference in how fully respondents are engaged. When it is possible, surveyors should personalize each salutation rather than use global salutations such as "Dear Respondent," "Dear Resident," or "Dear _____ Member"; a personalized greeting increases the respondent's sense of importance as a respondent. We were unable to personalize the salutations in our letters in the Workplace Assault Study because of insufficient resources. We were, however, able to personalize each outside envelope with the respondent's name and home address.

PURPOSE OF THE STUDY

All materials aimed at motivating respondents should clearly explain the purpose of the study. Again, see the three letters in Figures 3.8 through 3.10. In the advance letter (Figure 3.8), we specified the study's purpose in the second paragraph. In the final version of the cover letter (Figure 3.10), we specified the purpose in the first paragraph:

> Little is really known about personal safety and security while at work. The Service Employees International Union, Local [660/535] is concerned about the risks its members may encounter on a day-to-day basis. In cooperation with . . . , we are conducting a study of workplace safety.

In the original cover letter (Figure 3.9), we also specified the purpose in the first paragraph, but during the pretest, we discovered problems that led us to soften and modify the stated purpose of the letter, as we have described in Chapter 3. We also decided to shorten the introductory information in response to union officials' suggestions that we were providing too much information and that respondents were unlikely to read and comprehend so much verbiage. We present both versions of the cover letter here to illustrate the kinds of changes we made.

REASONS AN INDIVIDUAL'S PARTICIPATION IS IMPORTANT

Materials intended to motivate respondents should explain why each individual's participation is important. In our final cover letter in the Workplace Assault Study (Figure 3.10), we gave this information in the first and last sentences of the first paragraph:

> **We need your help to improve personal safety on the job for Los Angeles County employees.** . . . Results from this survey will help determine measures that could be taken to protect our members.

These sentences reiterate statements made in the advance letter (Figure 3.8), where we told potential respondents, **"Your participation in the survey is very important,"** and the information we were seeking **"has to come from you!"**

In the cover letter we used for the pretest, we included an additional reason for the importance of each individual's participation: the fact that it *was* a pretest. In the second paragraph of that letter, we stated, "Based on your comments and suggestions, the questionnaire will be revised"; as we have already noted, we did indeed make revisions after the pretest.

INCENTIVES TO ENCOURAGE RESPONDENT PARTICIPATION

Incentives used to encourage respondent participation often overlap with information about the purpose of the study and how the respondent was selected for the study. That was the case in the Workplace Assault Study. In the final cover letter (Figure 3.10), we explained:

> Only a small proportion of Los Angeles County employees has been selected to participate, so your experiences and thoughts on the subject are very important. **You will be representing many employees who are similar to yourself.**

We also noted that the information gathered in the study would be used to improve workplace safety. We included similar information in the advance letter (Figure 3.8):

> The results of this study will document the extent and nature of risks that our members encounter at work. Hopefully, future projects will address policies and practices intended to improve personal safety of . . . Los Angeles County workers.

Surveyors can motivate potential respondents to participate in survey studies in many ways. Response rates are always highest when the subject matter of the study has some personal relevance for the respondents, or when respondents believe that by participating they are contributing to some other, greater good. These are the techniques we used in the Workplace Assault Study.

Monetary or Material Incentives

Sometimes surveyors provide monetary or other material incentives (small gifts such as pencils or pens, notepads, calendars, or raffle tickets) to encourage potential respondents to participate and thus increase response rates. Some surveyors prefer to enclose an incentive gift with the first mailing, to encourage the potential respondent to complete and return the questionnaire; others use the promise of a gift as an inducement to respond, telling the potential respondent that a gift will be sent once the completed questionnaire is received.

When surveyors use raffle chances or lottery tickets as incentives, the winners are chosen from among those who responded. Many online market research surveys use this kind of incentive, automatically entering respondents in some form of drawing when they complete questionnaires. In those cases, the surveyors can easily contact the respondents who win through their e-mail addresses. When using e-mail addresses for such notification is not practical, surveyors can ask respondents to provide other contact information. If a surveyor wishes to provide incentives to all respondents and does not have contact information for them, he or she may need to collect this information as part of the survey. In such a case, the surveyor must guarantee that the information is secure and that every respondent's identity is protected.

There is some controversy among survey researchers over the use of material incentives to increase response rates. Some believe that the data collected from individuals who receive such incentives are unreliable. These surveyors reason that the use of incentives "buys" responses from individuals who normally would not respond and who will pay little or no attention to the import of the study when filling out the questionnaire, merely putting down any answers. Other surveyors feel that the use of incentives is entirely appropriate; indeed, in some circumstances, it is the only way to obtain a satisfactory response rate. These surveyors argue that material incentives serve merely to assure respondents that the surveyors believe their time is valuable and worth compensation.

Whether or not to use material incentives is up to the individual surveyor. If you elect to use such incentives in a mail survey, you must also decide whether to send them with all first attempts or give them only to those individuals who participate (i.e., return completed questionnaires). If you decide to use an incentive other than cash, you must give some consideration to the appropriateness of the gift.

Other Forms of Motivation

We are sure that surveyors have utilized an infinite variety of other methods in their efforts to motivate respondents and increase response rates. In the Workplace Assault Study, we added a cover flyer to the mailing of the questionnaire (see Figure 3.11). We developed the flyer as a result of the pilot test and at the suggestion of union officials. Our reasoning was that many potential respondents would not take sufficient time to read the cover letter and so would not be motivated by the information provided there. The purpose of the flyer was to catch the potential respondent's attention. Notice that the flyer used large and varied print, contained an appeal to respondents that emphasized what we perceived to be a common concern among members of the sample (namely, workplace safety), briefly emphasized the purpose of the study, and referenced the union.

We had the flyer printed on canary-yellow paper to catch the potential respondent's eye. As noted earlier, we do not recommend using such colors for questionnaires or cover letters because they make it too difficult for a respondent to read for any period of time; however, such colors can be used productively for occasional emphasis and to catch the attention of potential respondents.

Sometimes surveyors try to motivate respondents by offering to supply them with abbreviated reports of the survey results. Many respondents enjoy being able to compare their answers to the results and like knowing that they are part of a research project. Offering this form of incentive is a relatively inexpensive means of increasing response rates. However, surveyors should not offer such rewards if there is any chance that they might not be able to provide them, or if the results will not be known until so far in the future that respondents won't remember participating in the study.

USE OF ADVANCE LETTERS

Occasionally, surveyors find it profitable to send letters or place telephone calls to selected respondents in advance of mailing the questionnaires. Although this usually is not possible in group self-administered situations, there are instances in which surveyors can inform individuals that they will be asked to take part in a study at some future date. For example, employers can notify workers or teachers can tell students that they will be part of a study at a particular time and place and give them an idea of the study purpose. When surveyors use advance letters or telephone calls, these tools should serve the purpose of introducing the study and giving some brief information about it while alerting the respondents that they have been chosen to be among the special individuals who will receive a mailing within a few days.

We made the decision to use an advance letter in the Workplace Assault Study (see Figure 3.8) as a result of what we learned in the pilot study.

HOW MATERIAL INCENTIVES
WILL BE PROVIDED OR DISTRIBUTED

When surveyors tell respondents, in advance letters or cover letters, about material incentives being offered for study participation, they must also specify the processes by which those incentives will be distributed. In the Workplace Assault Study, the question of whether or not to use monetary or material incentives was moot; we simply did not have sufficient resources to consider this option. In another study conducted by a UCLA professor, $50 was awarded by lottery to four students who returned questionnaires in a survey that examined the social attitudes of American college students and compared them with those of peers in other countries. The cover letter was headed "WIN $50!!" and the procedure was described in the body of the letter as follows:

As an added incentive, we will award $50 each to four students returning a completed questionnaire. The winning students will be chosen at random from the pool of those returning a fully completed questionnaire to us. In order to award the $50 prizes, we need to know which students returned the questionnaire and which students did not. To ensure confidentiality, this information will not be associated with the students' questionnaires. To accomplish this, you will place your completed questionnaire inside of the plain, unmarked envelope and mail this envelope to us. You will notice that the larger envelope has a number in the lower left-hand corner. This will tell us that you have returned a questionnaire. At this point your outer envelope will be destroyed and the inner envelope containing your completed questionnaire will be placed in a separate pile. Thus, it will not be possible to associate a given name with a given questionnaire. Your confidentiality will then be assured.

Notice that these instructions provide explicit information about how the surveyors planned to ensure respondents' confidentiality while still allowing for provision of a cash incentive.

REALISTIC ESTIMATE OF THE TIME REQUIRED
TO COMPLETE THE QUESTIONNAIRE

The surveyor should provide potential respondents with a direct or indirect **estimate of the time** required to complete the questionnaire. If the surveyor has determined just how long an *average respondent* takes to complete the questionnaire and the questionnaire is relatively short, he or she can provide a direct estimate of the time needed. We stress *average respondent* here because people differ, both in the amount of time they take and in whether they complete the questionnaire at one sitting or over multiple sittings. If the surveyor gives a direct time estimate, he or she should clearly indicate that it represents only an average, and that some respondents will take less time and some will take more time. The surveyor should not attempt to give a direct estimate of time needed until the questionnaire has been thoroughly pretested and pilot work has been completed. As we mentioned earlier, some online questionnaires include progress indicators on each screen to provide respondents with information about how far along they are in their progress through the questionnaire.

When the surveyor anticipates that the questionnaire may take a relatively long time to complete or may require respondents to invest considerable thought, he or she will usually find it best to indicate the probable time needed in an indirect way. This is what we chose to do in both the Workplace Assault Study and the PERK Study. In the cover letter for the assault study (Figure 3.10), we itemized the kinds of information we were seeking to collect—namely, the type of work the respondent does and the place where he or she works, personal safety measures at the respondent's work site, how safe or unsafe the respondent feels at work, and the respondent's experience with workplace threats and assaults. We then went on to ask the respondent to participate: "Please take the time to complete the questionnaire and return it in the enclosed self-addressed stamped envelope." In the PERK Study (Figure 3.5), we itemized the kinds of information to be collected in the introduction to the questionnaire. In the third paragraph, we assured respondents that "we have arranged for you to have enough time to finish the questionnaire before we start your vision testing."

We decided to use indirect ways of indicating the length of time needed to complete the questionnaires in both of these studies, but for somewhat different reasons. In the Workplace Assault Study, we knew that those who had experienced assaults or threats would take significantly longer to complete the questionnaire, but we also knew that the "average" respondent would not have had such experiences and would therefore not need a lot of time. Thus the range of time needed across the sample was broad but skewed toward less time. In contrast, in the PERK Study, we knew from prior experience that respondents would take about 25-30 minutes to complete the questionnaire; the respondents also knew that. Because we were careful to provide respondents with adequate time and resources for completing the questionnaire, we saw no reason to state a time estimate in the introduction.

HOW AND WHY THE RESPONDENT WAS CHOSEN

Any materials intended to motivate respondents should tell them how and why they were chosen to participate in the survey. Respondents are chosen in many different ways. The Workplace Assault Study used **simple random sampling** after union lists were prestratified according to job classification. Ten strata were created, and either 175 or 188 union members were selected from each stratum regardless of the number of persons in it. For purposes of the cover letter, we did not need to attempt to explain **stratified sampling** to the respondents or exactly how randomization was achieved. It *was* important that we emphasize that only some union members were being asked to complete the questionnaire, that these persons had been selected randomly, and that their responses were important because they represented others like themselves. We included this information in the first two sentences of the advance letter (Figure 3.8) and then provided more detail in the second paragraph of the cover letter (Figure 3.10) as follows:

> You have been randomly selected from the membership list of Local [535's]660's Los Angeles County employees to participate in this survey. Only a small proportion of Los Angeles County employees has been selected to participate, so your experiences and thoughts on the subject are very important. **You will be representing many employees who are similar to yourself.**

In other studies, such as the PERK Study, everyone in a population receives the questionnaire. We briefly referenced this in the second paragraph of the introduction to the PERK questionnaire (Figure 3.5) as follows:

> In order to get accurate information about radial keratotomy and how it affects people's vision, we need information from **all** PERK patients. So please help us by answering the questions to the best of your ability.

EXPLANATION OF CONFIDENTIALITY AND HOW THE DATA WILL BE HANDLED

Both federal law and research ethics require that subjects of all research studies be provided with information about how the collected data will be used and how their privacy or the confidentiality of their data will be ensured. In studies using self-administered questionnaires, advance letters, cover letters, and introductory instructions provide the best occasions for conveying this information. Some studies collect truly **anonymous data** in that they do not collect personal information such as names, telephone numbers, or addresses from respondents, and thus make no effort to log responses or contact nonresponders. Where that is not the case—as in both of our two example studies, where we did have information about the respondents—surveyors must develop and follow procedures that will maintain the confidentiality of the data, and they must explain these procedures to potential respondents.

The confidentiality of information submitted over the Internet is of considerable concern to many users of the Web. Organizations that conduct online surveys must use the latest security measures and protocols so that they can assure their respondents that their sites are secure. Surveyors designing online surveys should begin their questionnaires with assurances of site security and guarantees that respondents' identities and any other information they provide online are protected.

As part of a long-term, ongoing study in which questionnaires were filled out at a clinical site, PERK respondents clearly were identifiable. Furthermore, during analyses, questionnaire data were linked to ophthalmic measures of vision. At the same time, it was important that we provide as much confidentiality and anonymity to respondents as possible within the requirements of the study. This was in our interests and in the interests of the respondents, to maximize the probabilities that respondents' answers were honest and complete. As we noted earlier, one of our major concerns in the PERK Study was to assure respondents that the information collected would not be available to personnel at the clinical site and would not affect their health care. In the last sentence in the questionnaire introduction (Figure 3.5), we told respondents how to return the questionnaire to us in a way that would ensure confidentiality: "When you are **finished** with the questionnaire, **seal** the questionnaire in the attached envelope and **leave it with** the clinical coordinator for the PERK Study."

In the Workplace Assault Study, we had had no prior contact with the respondents, so we emphasized the confidentiality of the data in the cover letter, clearly specifying that no information would be released to the respondent's employer (see Figure 3.10). Furthermore, we increased confidence in our assurances of confidentiality by sending the questionnaires to respondents' home addresses (rather than their workplaces) and by having them return the questionnaires to UCLA rather than to the union offices. We were unable to guarantee anonymity from the research staff because we did indeed plan to follow up on nonrespondents. We also included questions at the end of the questionnaire that asked for volunteers for follow-up interviews and included code numbers on the outside of all return envelopes.

PROVISION OF A NAME AND PHONE NUMBER TO CALL FOR INFORMATION

The surveyor must always provide respondents with a name and phone number of someone who will be available to answer questions about the questionnaire. This person should be accessible and should be able to answer questions, send additional copies of the questionnaire, or respond to other requests respondents may have. Often, this will be the person (or persons) who signs the cover letter. In the case of the Workplace Assault Study, we provided respondents with the names and phone numbers of two people: One was Deborah Riopelle, the project manager who was located at UCLA; the other was a member of the union staff whose name the respondents would recognize. In the case of an online survey, the surveyor should provide respondents with an e-mail address they can use to submit questions about the study or its sponsors. If the survey team will be unable to answer e-mail requests for information quickly, giving respondents a toll-free telephone number to call is a good alternative.

There are always potential respondents who will call to verify the purpose or sponsorship of a study, to assure themselves that the organization is legitimate or that confidentiality will be maintained. Other potential respondents will have questions about the content of the questionnaire or how their names were selected for the sample. If the surveyor fails to provide respondents with a name and number they can call, the respondents are unlikely to complete and return the questionnaire. We recommend that, whenever possible, the surveyor offer respondents the option of calling the project collect. Unfortunately, this was not possible in the Workplace Assault Study because telephones within the University of California system cannot be set up to accept collect calls, and we were unable to provide an off-campus number for respondents to contact.

WHEN AND HOW TO RETURN THE QUESTIONNAIRE

Although surveyors need to let respondents know how quickly they should return their completed questionnaires, including a deadline for return of the questionnaire in the cover letter can work to the surveyor's disadvantage. Whereas some respondents may be motivated by a deadline to complete the form and return it immediately, others may set the packet aside initially and then, upon picking it up close to or after the deadline, believe that it is too late to respond. In the Workplace Assault Study, we attempted to go between the horns of this dilemma by giving a deadline date but providing latitude in the way we stated it. For example, "It would be very helpful to have your completed questionnaire returned to us by January 25, 1995."

In addition, the surveyor needs to tell respondents *how* they should return the questionnaire. In most mail surveys, the surveyor includes a preaddressed, postage-paid envelope in the questionnaire packet for this purpose and includes instructions in the cover letter telling the respondent to return the questionnaire "in the enclosed self-addressed stamped envelope." However, as we mentioned earlier, respondents often misplace these envelopes, so we strongly recommend that the surveyor include the survey project office's address at the end of the questionnaire itself.

Online surveys can have a time advantage over mail surveys in terms of the field period (assuming a questionnaire protocol already exists or is simple to set up). An investigator conducting an online survey does not have to allow for time for mail delivery to and from respondents, so those extra days can be allocated to ongoing data collection, or the study period can simply be shortened. Online surveys also have the advantage of requiring little data processing at the end of the study period, because the data are entered and "cleaned" electronically in real time as they are collected. Results can be available in a matter of hours after the conclusion of data collection if the programs for data retrieval are developed before data collection begins. However, the ability to get results so quickly can vary with the complexity of the questionnaire design and the quality of the programming.

Checklist for Motivating Respondents and Writing Cover Letters

✓ Explain the purpose of the study.

✓ Describe who is sponsoring the study.

✓ Consider sending advance letters.

✓ Consider using other methods, such as newsletters or flyers, to publicize the study.

✓ Include a cover letter with the questionnaire.

- Use letterhead.

- Date the letter to be consistent with the actual date of mailing or administration.

- Provide a name and phone number for the respondent to contact for further information.

- Personalize the salutation, if feasible.

- Maximize the attractiveness and readability of the letter.

✓ Explain how the respondent was chosen and why his or her participation is important.

✓ Explain when and how to return the questionnaire.

✓ Describe incentives, if used.

✓ Directly or indirectly provide a realistic estimate of the time required by the average respondent to complete the questionnaire.

✓ Explain how the confidentiality of the respondent's data will be protected.

✓ Determine whether and how a deadline date will be provided for returning the questionnaire.

Writing Questionnaire Specifications

Once the surveyor has finalized the questionnaire, he or she needs to write the **questionnaire specifications.** This first major documentation of the study should include information on the study's objectives, who the respondents were, how the questionnaire was administered, how follow-up was conducted, how completed questionnaires were processed, and the reason each question or set of questions was included in the questionnaire.

Novice surveyors frequently feel that once they have completed the design and administration of a study, they cannot possibly forget any detail of its creation or the decisions made during the study period, but in fact, substantial amounts of time can pass before collected data are actually analyzed or written up. Sometimes, surveyors run out of money and cannot complete their studies in a timely fashion. Sometimes, other competing activities or research projects necessitate the postponement of a study's completion. Sometimes, the people originally involved in a study leave the organization to take other jobs. We personally know of situations where it has taken as long as 10 years for a study to be completed. Even when such interruptions do not occur, it behooves the conscientious surveyor to document the decisions made during the construction and administration of the questionnaire. At minimum, questionnaire specifications should include information about the objective of the study, the selection and tracking of the sample, the number and timing of administrations and follow-up procedures, and the sources and reasons for each question.

When questionnaires are administered by interview, "interviewer specifications" are usually extracted out of the questionnaire specifications; these are used in training interviewers, and interviewers also use them as reference guides in the field.

OBJECTIVE OF THE STUDY

The questionnaire specifications should briefly summarize the purpose of the study. The specifications for the PERK Study stated the objectives of the questionnaire as follows:

> The 10-year questionnaire has three objectives. First, it allows us to get systematic information from patients at all the nine sites about problems they might have had, their current vision, and the current lens-wearing patterns. Second, it allows us to compare patients with themselves at baseline and at 1, 2, and 6 years after radial keratotomy on their first eye. Third, it allows us to compare the health of PERK patients to other, more representative samples of the United States' population.

Notice that the questionnaire had three objectives. The first objective was one that necessitated the collection of "new" or original data from this questionnaire, but the second and third objectives implied that some of the questions on the questionnaire would be adopted or adapted from past PERK questionnaires or other sources that would enable us to compare the data collected with existing data sets. The specification of these three objectives alerted the reader to the kinds of questions that would be asked and the fact that some of the questions on this questionnaire would not be original but drawn from other studies.

SELECTION AND TRACKING OF THE SAMPLE

The questionnaire specifications should describe in detail the selection and **tracking** of the survey sample. For example, in the PERK Study, the questionnaire was given to *all* participants in the clinical trial as soon as they entered the clinical center for their 10-year examination. No effort was made to administer to patients who did not come in for this follow-up examination. In contrast, in the Workplace Assault Study, union personnel randomly selected between 175 and 188 members from each of 10 job categories in the two locals.[1] This resulted in 1,763 names. Insufficient addresses existed for 19 of these names, so they were immediately eliminated from the sample. On January 5 and 6, 1995, advance letters were sent to the remaining 1,744 persons. On January 17, 1995, a packet containing the questionnaire, a cover letter, a flyer, and an envelope for returning the questionnaire was mailed to each of the same 1,744 persons, which we considered our sample. On January 24, 1995, reminder postcards were sent to all of these persons, regardless of whether or not they had returned the questionnaire (see Figure 3.7 in Chapter 3). Then, on March 4 through 6, 1995, a second questionnaire with a new cover letter was sent to each of the 1,143 persons who had failed to respond to our first two mailings but for whom addresses appeared to be correct. The new cover letter (see Figure 4.2) repeated some of the same information given before but included a new section that emphasized the importance of our getting responses from people who were *not* assaulted or who did *not* perceive their workplaces to be unsafe. Finally, in April 1995, we began contacting by telephone those who still had not responded.

SOCIAL SERVICES
UNION

AMERICAN
FEDERATION
OF NURSES

309 SO. RAYMOND
AVENUE
PASADENA
CALIFORNIA
91105
818-796-0051
FAX 818-796-2335

February 21, 1995

Dear Member,

About four weeks ago we sent you a questionnaire about personal safety and security while at work. As of today, we have not yet received your completed questionnaire.

The Service Employees International Union, Local 535 is conducting this study of workplace safety in cooperation with the Southern California Injury Prevention Research Center at UCLA because of concerns members have expressed about personal safety while at work. Results from this survey will help determine measures that could be taken to protect Local 535 members.

You may feel that because your safety at work has not been threatened you don't need to reply. This is not true. By hearing about the experiences of all Local 535 members we can develop a better idea of which situations are safer than others. We are writing to you again because of the importance **each** questionnaire has to the study. **We need your completed questionnaire.**

We recognize how busy you must be and greatly appreciate you taking the time to complete this questionnaire. If by chance you did not receive the first questionnaire or it got misplaced, we have enclosed a replacement. It would be very helpful to have your completed questionnaire returned to us by **March 3, 1995.**

<u>**Your responses are confidential.**</u> **No names or individual information will be used or released to your employer.** If you have any questions or concerns, please feel free to call Deborah Riopelle, M.S.P.H. at UCLA, (310) 555-4053 or Wilma Cadorna at Local 535 at 818-555-0051.

Sincerely,

Jerry L. Clyde
President, Social Services Chapter
SEIU Local 535

Linda Bourque, Ph.D.
UCLA School of Public Health

Figure 4.2.   Example of a Cover Letter Directed to Respondents as Part of a Second Full Mailing (Nonresponders)

All of the above information, starting with how the sample was selected and why it was selected that way and ending with response rates by time of contact and job category, is documented in the questionnaire specifications. Thus, when we get ready to analyze and write up our findings, we can quickly go to the specifications to refresh our memories about how and why we selected the sample we did, the kind of response we obtained at each stage of the mailing, and the extent to which response rates differed by job stratum.

TIMING OF ADMINISTRATION

The questionnaire specifications should also include detailed information about the *timing* of contacts with the sample, as illustrated in the description of the Workplace Assault Study contacts above. In the PERK Study, the questionnaire was given out only once, and every effort was made to ensure that clinic personnel obtained a completed questionnaire from each respondent. In contrast, in the Workplace Assault Study, respondents were contacted a minimum of three times (advance letter, first mailing of questionnaire, and follow-up postcard) and a maximum of five or more times (advance letter, first mailing of questionnaire, follow-up postcard, second mailing of questionnaire, and one or more phone calls).

By keeping track of *when* respondents respond relative to the timing and number of the contacts, the surveyor can assess various things about the sample. In the Workplace Assault Study, for example, we were able to assess whether responsiveness varied with job category, gender, age, perceptions of vulnerability in the workplace, or actual experiences of physical assault.

INSTRUCTIONS FOR ADMINISTERING QUESTIONS

The specifications need to include any instructions provided for persons who administer the questionnaire. Once the timing and method of contacting respondents had been specified for the Workplace Assault Study, no further administrative requirements had to be outlined in the specifications. In contrast, in the PERK Study, the specifications contained instructions to the clinical coordinator for administering the questionnaire as follows:

ADMINISTRATION OF THE QUESTIONNAIRE

TIME: Allow at least 30 minutes for the patient to fill out the questionnaire. If you interview any patients over the phone, make sure that they have the time to do it. You may want to call them and arrange a special time for you to conduct the interview.

SITE: Provide each patient with a quiet room or secluded area in the general waiting room. Provide them with a pencil or pen, table or clipboard, and the envelope in which to put the completed questionnaire.

OTHER PEOPLE: Discourage other people from "helping" the patient fill out the questionnaire. If you interview them, try to do it at a time when they will not be interrupted by family or colleagues and at a time when they have no other things to do.

EMPHASIZE: We want to know about **their experiences** with radial keratotomy and how they feel about things. There are no "right" or "wrong" answers, and patients should not try to please you with the answer they give. We **expect** to find variations in opinions and experiences.

In general, remember that **we need their opinions** of their vision, not our observations about what we think their vision is. Please give them enough time to think about their answers and avoid hurrying them through the questionnaire. If patients do not like our alternatives, encourage them to write down their feelings or experiences and we will evaluate the information they provide.

COVER PAGE: The cover page provides the patient with a brief description of the information that the questionnaire is designed to collect. As you give the questionnaire to the patient, direct his or her attention to the second and third paragraphs in particular. These describe how the data will be used and tell the patient what to do when he or she has completed the questionnaire.

COORDINATOR: Before giving the questionnaire to the patient, please make sure that the patient's identification number is on every page of the questionnaire and that the date of administration is filled out on the cover page.

Notice that the above instructions are formatted in a way that makes it easy for the survey administrator to find information on a particular subject, and that every effort is made to encourage the clinic coordinator *not* to interfere with the patient while he or she is filling out the questionnaire. This is particularly important when the persons administering a questionnaire are not professional interviewers. In the same way surveyors must try to recognize and compensate for their own biases, they also need to try to anticipate the biases of others who may be involved in the collection of data.

QUESTIONS RAISED BY RESPONDENTS

The questionnaire specifications should also include any other information given to data collectors about administration of the questionnaire, including information on what they should do in response to respondent questions. Just as surveyors must attempt to anticipate the attitudes and behaviors of data collectors, they need to try to anticipate questions or challenges that respondents may direct to data collectors. Whenever possible, surveyors should provide data collectors with information that will help them answer such questions or handle such challenges. The following information was included in the specifications for the PERK Study:

QUESTIONS RAISED
BY THE PATIENT

Questions asked about the questionnaire will probably be of two types: a question of clarification or a question designed to have you provide the information or your opinion about their vision.

CLARIFICATION: If a patient does not understand a question, try to find out what it is that he or she does not understand and try to find a synonym or another way to say it. Please make a note of the question asked and let Portia Griffin at Emory know about it.

NO APPROPRIATE ANSWER AVAILABLE: If a patient cannot represent him/herself with the answers available, tell him or her to write down an answer that **does** represent his or her feelings or experiences.

CHALLENGES: If a subject starts to challenge the objective of the questionnaire or a particular item in it, or says that it is repetitive, etc., please listen, be polite, and be noncommittal. **Do not give** patients the answers or indicate that you will let them stop answering the questions.

SOURCES AND REASONS FOR QUESTIONS

The major historical purpose of questionnaire specifications has been to document the sources of and reasons for including the questions or sets of questions in the instrument. Figure 4.3 provides an example of the specifications from the PERK Study, which describes Questions 2 through 12 (see Figure 3.1, Chapter 3), Questions 43 through 45, and Questions 54 through 61 (see Figure 3.3).

PERK 10-Year Questionnaire
August 17, 1992

LENS-WEARING PATTERNS:

Q2-25 Questions 2-25 ask patients to tell us about their current lens-wearing patterns.

Q2-7 Questions 2-7 were used in both the baseline and 6-year questionnaires to measure patients' functional vision. These questions are similar to questions used in RAND's Health Insurance Experiment and a wide range of other studies where vision has been assessed. We are repeating them so that we can see what kind of effect radial keratotomy has had on their functional vision. The questions on presbyopia and distant vision that were added to Question 1 above represent an effort to improve the precision of information traditionally collected exclusively with Questions 6 and 7.

Q8 In evaluating how presbyopia affects the eyes of persons who have had radial keratotomy, we realized that we have no way of identifying patients who might have been presbyopic at baseline. Question 8 provides an opportunity to get a rough estimate of this.

Q9-13 Questions 9-13 assess whether patients have become or are becoming presbyopic and how presbyopia is affecting both their vision and their use of lenses. These questions can also be used in assessing how severe overcorrection affects the daily vision of PERK patients.

Q9 Ascertains whether the patient was told about presbyopia in the context of the PERK Study.

Q10 Ascertains whether the patient is presbyopic and whether presbyopia has necessitated the use of spectacles for near vision.

Q11 Ascertains when presbyopia resulted in the use of spectacles.

Q12 A number of situations are listed in Question 12. Patients are asked to respond for **each eye.** By looking at the pattern of responses to Question 12, we will be able to assess to what degree patients are disabled by presbyopia or severe overcorrection of their vision.

.
.
.
.

Figure 4.3a. Example of Questionnaire Specifications

Q43-45   These three questions were in both the baseline and 6-year questionnaires. Originally included in RAND's Health Insurance Experiment, data obtained with these questions were reported in Borque, Rubenstein, Cosand et al., Psychological characteristics of candidates for the Prospective Evaluation of Radial Keratotomy, Archives of Ophthalmology 1984; 102:1187-1192. Inclusion of these questions will allow us to compare the patients both to themselves at earlier points in time and to RAND myopes.

.
.
.
.
.

Q54-65   Questions 54-65 provide us with information about how and when PERK patients use their eyes to read, drive, watch television, and participate in sports and other physical activities. The number and type of activities done as well as the time of day at which they are done may influence their need for and use of lenses.

Figure 4.3b.   Example of Questionnaire Specifications

Notice that specifications may be provided for sets of questions (e.g., Q2-25), subsets of questions (Q2-7, Q9-13, Q43-45, and Q54-65), or individual questions (e.g., Q9, Q10, Q11, and Q12). Each specification describes the purpose of the question (or questions) and whether it replicates or revises an earlier question or, by implication, is a new question. For example, Questions 2 through 7 replicate questions that were asked in earlier PERK questionnaires and the RAND Health Insurance Experiment. In contrast, Questions 9 through 13 are new to this questionnaire because this is the first time we are assessing presbyopia (the decreased ability to see things that are close that occurs in middle age).

Questions 43 through 45 also replicate questions that were used in other PERK questionnaires and in the HIE. In the case of these questions, however, data collected were reported in an earlier article. The fact that this occurred is documented as part of the specification, and a complete citation is provided for the article. This reminds the surveyor at a later time that earlier analyses had occurred and provides a quick reference as to where he or she can find information about them.

In general, if the surveyor cannot explain in a specification *why* a question is included in the questionnaire, there probably is no reason for it to be there.

Checklist for Writing Questionnaire Specifications

✓ Briefly describe the objective of the study.

✓ Describe the study sample and response rates.

✓ Describe any tracking done of the sample.

✓ Describe the timing of data collection and tracking.

✓ Provide instructions for administering questionnaires.

✓ Provide answers for data collectors to use in response to anticipated questions.

✓ Describe why each question is asked.

✓ If questions are adopted or adapted from other studies, explain the reasons for such decisions and provide complete citations to the other studies.

✓ Index the specifications for easy reference.

Note

1. Nine strata were selected from Local 660, the largest local, and 175 names were randomly selected within each stratum. The populations of the groups at the time of the sample draw were as follows: Public Social Services, 6,208; Public Health Department, 1,336; Public Library, 309; Probation, 578; Sheriff's Department, 908; Parks and Recreation, Animal Care and Control, and Public Works, 922; Assessor's Office, Children's Services, and Treasurer and Tax Collector Offices, 1,625; Municipal and Superior Courts, 1,067; and Hospitals, 3,501. Only 3,221 members of Local 535 worked in Los Angeles County, with the largest group being the 2,090 in the Department of Social Services; 188 persons were randomly selected from this stratum.

5 Implementation

 The **implementation** of mail and other self-administered surveys requires considerable coordination and attention to detail. This multistage process begins with sample selection and ends with the processing of the last of the returned and completed questionnaires. In this chapter, we discuss issues associated with the identification and selection of the sample as well as the material costs and staffing needs associated with mail and other self-administered surveys. We elaborate on the processes involved in the coordination of self-administered surveys; in the case of mail surveys, these include preparation of packets for mailing, the posting of these packets, subsequent follow-up and return of packets, and the tracking of envelopes that are returned because of address problems. We provide examples of expected expenditures and person hours based on actual surveys.

 We do not discuss the implementation of online surveys here, although this method is rapidly gaining in popularity for surveys that are limited to samples with ready access to the Internet. Online survey methods are technologically and methodologically quite different from paper-and-pencil methods in design and execution; we cannot possibly provide adequate guidance on the administration of such surveys within the space constraints of this chapter.

We should mention, however, the new dimension that online surveys add to issues of sampling, in particular concerning how surveyors contact and inform intended respondents and how those persons can gain access to surveys. For some studies, surveyors' contacts with respondents can be accomplished through e-mail invitations (if the surveyors have the appropriate e-mail addresses). Alternatively, surveyors can send potential respondents advance letters through the traditional mail system, inviting them to participate and directing them to the survey Web site (again, the surveyors must have the addresses of the intended respondents). Surveyors interested in less targeted samples can buy e-mail addresses or the street addresses of household Internet subscribers from sample contracting firms, or they might place links in suitable Web sites so that individuals logged on to those sites can see their invitations or banners, click on the links, and take the surveys (either of these options represents an additional cost for the survey study). For example, if a surveyor wants to conduct an online survey with a subpopulation of persons who are more likely than others to read books, he or she might check into the possibility of contracting with a major online book dealer to carry the surveyor's invitation on the book dealer's Web site. Although a sample selected in such a way cannot be demonstrated to be representative of any particular population, it may be adequate for the purpose of the study being undertaken.

Developing and Producing the Sample

Typically, surveyors consider using self-administered surveys only when they are confident that their desired sample populations are accessible at designated locations. This survey methodology is often the only efficient means of obtaining data from somewhat rare populations (that is, populations made up of individuals who have characteristics that are not common in the general population). For example, say a major motorcycle manufacturer wants to test the acceptance of a new concept in handlebars among members of the motorcycle-riding public. The easiest approach might be to mail questionnaires to members of motorcycle clubs or hand out questionnaires to customers at large motorcycle distributorships or motorcycle repair shops.

A surveyor can further refine the characteristics of the groups sampled for self-administered questionnaires by being increasingly selective about the location of administration. For example, if the purpose of a study is to determine the types of baby products that mothers of infants purchase, the surveyor might arrange to have self-administered questionnaires handed out to parents in the waiting rooms of well-baby clinics. In short, surveyors can gather samples from many places, including waiting rooms, classrooms, places of employment, and residences, whether individual homes, group living situations (such as school dormitories), or temporary residences (such as hospital rooms). The samples used in self-administered surveys conducted in this manner are known as *convenience samples;* surveyors generally use such samples as a means of getting data easily and quickly from highly specialized populations. In many instances, self-administered surveys eliminate the need for surveyors to go to overwhelming effort, at high cost, to locate at random particular types of individuals within the general population.

Surveyors often use mail surveys when their sample populations are made up of members of particular professional, political, religious, or social organizations; employees within particular institutions or job classifications; students; subscribers to particular newsletters and magazines; or consumers of particular products or services. Again, a major consideration in favor of using mail surveys is the appreciably lower cost of such surveys, compared with in-person or telephone interview surveys, for locating appropriate populations.

Surveyors do not always choose to use mail or other self-administered surveys because of the ease of finding rare populations, however. Frequently, they choose this method because it is far less expensive than telephone or in-person surveys. Additionally, mail surveys can sometimes be more successful at getting data from hard-to-reach populations, such as doctors, business executives, and politicians.

If you are evaluating the use of certain sources for a mail survey sample, you need to be aware of potential problems. For example, if you use addresses and/or names and addresses obtained from telephone directories, you need to take into account the approximate mobility of the population under consideration and the rate of unlisted households in the area. If you are mailing questionnaires to specific names in the telephone book, you need to determine the rate of turnover in telephone number ownership (that is, how many people are likely to have changed their telephone numbers) by the time you use the directory for a sample. Obviously, out-of-date listings will result in undelivered or unanswered mail.

If you are generating a sample from a telephone directory, you would also be wise to contact your local telephone company to find out the proportion of households with unlisted numbers in the area covered by the directory. If a number is not listed, that household will have no opportunity to be included in the survey; people with unlisted phone numbers will therefore be underrepresented in the population. If having an unlisted telephone number is typical of people with particular characteristics, such as the elderly, those with a high income, or single females, your sample will be biased away from that portion of the population. In some cities, such as Los Angeles, the unlisted rate is around 60% of households, whereas in less urban areas, the rate can drop below 20%. A different twist on this problem is households with telephone numbers listed in the directory but with the street addresses suppressed. Regardless of the source of your sample, you should always try to determine how the sample might be biased due to lack of inclusion.

SAMPLE AVAILABILITY

When surveyors plan to conduct self-administered surveys in group settings, they must obtain permission to access the populations from the institutions where these individuals are. If, for example, we want to hand out questionnaires to mothers of infants at well-baby clinics, we need permission from the authorities who oversee those establishments to approach their clients. Likewise, if we want to contact members of a motorcycle club, we need to be granted access to those individuals by someone at the executive level of the club; if we want to approach customers at motorcycle dealerships or repair shops, we need permission to do so from the business owners. In some instances, before an organization can grant access to a surveyor, the organization itself may be required to obtain informed consent from the individuals to be studied.

In most cases in which surveyors are preparing to conduct mail surveys, they need to gain access to the names and addresses of the individuals in the populations they want to sample. Organizations often have such information stored and available in some electronic medium, but surveyors obviously cannot access these files without proper authorization. They must seek permission to use such data files from the organizations.

The fees that organizations charge surveyors for access to sample information can vary considerably. If you are seeking such information from groups or organizations that are either sponsoring the research or interested in the results, you may simply be asked to cover the costs of materials (e.g., labels and machine time). Sometimes, you may have to pay for both the labor and the materials required to program and process your request. When you are seeking sample information from the organization sponsoring the research, the cooperating organization may provide the labels free of charge (such an organization often may also help to defray part or all of the mailing costs). Typically, the organization should be able to provide you with either addressed mailing labels or raw data on some computer medium.

There are publishing companies that specialize in the compilation and production of directories of government officials and employees, corporate officials, business firms within professions, and the like. If your research is focused on individuals with particular sociodemographic or socio-economic characteristics, you might decide to purchase a sample from such a directory publisher, or from a commercial bulk-mailing establishment or a specialized marketing firm. These kinds of organizations compile mailing addresses within certain demographic domains. Often, they link U.S. Census data to zip codes, so that samples can be focused on neighborhoods where households with particular characteristics are more likely to exist, such as married senior citizens with annual incomes over $30,000. Many organizations involved in providing address samples supplement the data with information they have gathered from other sources, such as sales profiles from department and grocery stores, newspaper readership, and other surveys conducted in the area.

In today's computer-dominated environment, it often seems that an amazing (and at times disconcerting) amount of information is easily available about any individual. When using purchased samples, however, you need to keep in mind that the data are not necessarily representative of the general population and may be subject to innumerable biases.

List samples can often be unreliable. They may be out-of-date—that is, they may not have current address and/or telephone number information on individuals—or they may not contain all the candidates possible for inclusion in the study. Lists can be up-to-date and inclusive and still contain clerical errors that will cause problems when you try to reach respondents. It is always a good idea to spot-check your sample before using it—for example, by mailing to a few addresses on the list, making some telephone calls to numbers on the list, or comparing list information to another source, such as the telephone directory.

SELECTING THE SAMPLE

When administering a questionnaire at a site such as a grocery store, you may want to ask all individuals encountered to fill out the form, or you may want to select a subsample of these individuals. If you decide on a subsample, you need to determine a means of selecting respondents representatively rather than taking only the first group to appear. Ideally, your sample should be spread out evenly over times of day, days of the week, or types of individuals.

A commonly used means of selecting respondents is to determine a sampling interval. For example, assume that 1,000 parents of infants come into the well-baby clinics in our sample in any given week. We have decided that we want to interview only 200 of them. To spread the sample across the entire week's population, we would approach every fifth client who comes for well-baby care. This is known as a *sampling interval*. This method of selection provides a systematically selected sample within a given time period and place.

If you are interested in a subgroup within the general sample population, such as people between 35 and 55 years of age or African Americans, you will want to select the respondents at different sampling intervals to ensure that you obtain data from a sufficient number of individuals for each group you want to compare. This is called *stratified systematic sampling*.

In some group settings, such as clinics or classrooms, you may be able to preselect respondents from patient charts or class rosters (after obtaining permission to view these records). If such lists are not available, you will have to determine another means of selecting respondents, such as the order in which they signed in or entered the room.

You can select a mailing sample by using essentially the same process. If you have a sample list but do not want to use the whole list (or universe), you must give instructions to the processor concerning how to select the sample using a sampling interval. When selecting or drawing samples, it is a common practice to start at a random starting point in the list and, using a constant interval, rotate from the bottom around to the top of the list and down to the initial starting point. If, for example, we have a list of 1,000 mothers who bring their babies to a clinic and we want to send questionnaires to 200, we select a random start point—say, woman number 322 on the list—and then take every fifth woman on the list from that point on (327, 332, 337, and so on). Again, if the data file contains individual data on characteristics of particular interest, you will want to draw the sample with different sampling intervals for different types of individuals.

ADDRESSING THE MAILING

There are three methods for putting the sample addresses on the mailing packets: The addresses can be handwritten directly on the envelopes, typed or printed directly on the envelopes, or typed or printed on labels that are then affixed to the envelopes. There has been some research indicating a nonsignificant increase in the rate of returns with hand-addressed envelopes. Similarly, machine-printed envelopes have been shown to be received a bit more favorably than those with labels affixed. Unless the sample size is extremely small—say, a few hundred—the intensive labor involved in hand-addressing envelopes does not warrant this approach. Similarly, if the sample file must be created by keyboarding, you would be wiser to make sure this clerical time is spent entering the information into a computer file so that it is available for subsequent mailings.

A final precaution: With much of the mail being optically scanned today, it is a good idea to check with your local post office to determine if there are any specific layout restrictions on bulk mailings. We once discovered that if more than four spaces occurred between the last number of the street address and the street name, the post office scanner stopped reading at the unit number and found the address "incomplete." When you lay out your data field for addressing, be sure that the address length and width conform to the size of your mailing labels.

PLANNING THE SAMPLE FILE

When you provide the specifications for the sample format or label layout, consider how many mailings you plan to send to each respondent. If the sample file is not easily accessible, you will want to have all the necessary materials run at the same time. For example, if you plan an initial mailing and two follow-ups, ask for three copies of the labels to be run along with a printout of the sample list. This will eliminate the need to return to the supplier and ask for additional label runs and will give you a master copy of the sample against which you can log in your returns. This will save you costs in the long run because a substantial part of the cost in running address labels is typically in the initial setup time or programming. Thus requesting additional sets of labels on the initial run adds to the cost of materials only, and not to the cost of labor. If for some reason you cannot obtain more than one set of address labels, you can make copies on label sheets on most photocopying machines if the original label format is a standard three addresses across.

If you are running the address labels from within your own organization and there is no problem with access, you should not run all the sets at one time. If you are going to have the postal service send back address corrections, or if you plan to track bad addresses, you will want to make these changes or corrections to your master file before you produce the next batch of labels. Additionally, if you are logging in completed returns, you will have eliminated labels for these respondents and for those who are lost to follow-up (deceased, no usable address, and so on).

Another thing you need to consider regarding label production is whether to use self-adhesive or preglued labels. If you are putting labels on by hand, self-adhesive labels are most practical. If the labels are to be affixed by machine, consult with your mailing coordinator to determine which kind of labels will work with the machine to be used for your mailing.

The final consideration for label production is how the materials are to be delivered. If the mailing is to be delivered by the U.S. Postal Service, you should specify that the sample address labels be run in zip code order. This is especially important if your mailing is large—say, 500 pieces or more. The U.S. Postal Service will discount postage on large mailings if your addresses are presorted by zip code.

If by some odd chance you are dealing with a sample that is not computerized—that is, it does not exist in an electronic format file—you may well find it to be cost- and time-effective to enter it into a computerized medium. When entering the address data or setting up the sample file, make sure the final file is accessible to a spreadsheet program or other software that will enable you to call up individual respondents on request. If you are going to log in your returns by individual, you will want to be able to call up the identification number of each case and preestablish locations where you can enter date of return and keep track of the type of outcome. By *outcome,* we mean what ultimately happened to the packet; some examples of outcomes are "moved and left no address," "no such address," "insufficient address," "respondent deceased," "refused to complete," and "completed questionnaire received."

You should run sample progress reports at predesignated intervals, such as once a week. These reports should compile the information in your file to document the total number of completed questionnaires, the number of questionnaires that were undeliverable, and the number yet to be resolved. Progress reports can be very extensive and elaborate, even including information on tracking progress variables such as telephone directory search initiated, Department of Motor

Vehicles search initiated, credit company search initiated (if being used), outcome for each type of search, date of initiation and outcome, and the name of the individual responsible for the search if more than one.

In the case of group administration, where you are unlikely to have a sample list, you will want to keep at least daily records of the number of completed questionnaires and, if you are sampling special populations, the numbers within each subgroup that have been completed. You should also keep a count of the number of individuals who have declined to participate.

ETHICS AND RESPONSIBILITIES

You must always keep respondent confidentiality foremost in your planning. You should maintain and store your sample information in a way that will prohibit persons other than study staff from gaining access to who, what, and where potential respondents are, or whether or not they have returned the survey. As is often the case, you may have individuals working on some aspect of your study who have never been exposed to survey research. It is incumbent on you to educate these employees on the protection of subjects and any information that may have been gathered about them.

Some kinds of work settings, such as hospitals, clinics, and schools, have established human subjects protection committees whose mandate is to review all research protocols and ensure that no harm can come to respondents if they participate in any research. Protecting the respondents and doing them no harm are the primary responsibilities of anyone who conducts a survey.

Another "standard" adopted by sincere surveyors is that of being honest about their intent. It is dishonest to solicit participation in any type of survey under one pretext and then use the survey to promote something else. Some surveyors will claim that they are not trying to sell any product or solicit money and then turn around and try to sell a product or solicit funds later in the interview. Sometimes, unethical surveyors seek information in interviews that is later used for follow-ups for solicitation. This is not only deceitful, it gives the entire profession of survey research a bad name.

SAMPLE SIZE

You need to take several factors into account when considering the size of your sample or the number of individuals or institutions to whom you will administer or send your questionnaire. Your first concern should be to determine how many completed responses you will need to demonstrate that your research hypothesis is correct. There are several easy-to-use publications available that provide basic survey sampling guidelines (see **How to Design Survey Studies** and **How to Sample in Surveys**, Volumes 6 and 7 in this series). If the number of individuals qualified to respond to your questionnaire is limited, you may need to survey the entire universe of individuals.

Once you have determined the minimally acceptable completed sample size (the number of filled-out, returned questionnaires), you can estimate the total sample size, or the number of individuals or addresses required to produce the desired number of usable returns. With self-administered questionnaires in group settings, sample loss occurs because individuals decline to participate, group turnout is lower than expected, or the materials are not distributed as directed. In mail surveys, there are two main causes of respondent loss that surveyors need to compensate for: bad addresses and nonresponse.

If the initial purpose of your mailing is to screen a population for particular characteristics, you will need to factor in the proportion of your overall population that you estimate will qualify and increase your mailing sample size accordingly. For example, say you have a list of all home owners in a particular area, but your primary focus is on home owners with minor children in their households. You will need to obtain an estimate of the proportion of owner-occupied homes with children under age 18 in residence and adjust your overall mailing size upward to account for the loss of owner-occupied homes without minor children.

All address lists are subject to attrition and error. Often, such lists are at least a year old. In some population types, residential and occupational mobility is extremely high. Also, many address files are based on information that was originally handwritten; therefore, the entry is subject to the interpretation of the individual typing in the data as well as the completeness of the information provided. Typing or entry errors are a final source of address error. It takes only one error in street address or zip code to render a piece of mail undeliverable.

Because address lists are prone to error, the next thing you must consider in determining your sample size is what proportion of names and/or addresses in your sample file will be unusable (i.e., will be deemed undeliverable by the U.S. Postal Service or other delivery service). Some of the reasons the U.S. Postal Service cites for nondelivery are "addressee unknown," "moved and left no forwarding address," "forwarding order has expired" (the postal service maintains forwarding address orders for one year, and no longer), "incomplete address," "no such address," and "refused delivery." You will need to estimate the proportion of the sample you will lose for all these reasons.

You may be able to get an estimate based on prior experience from the supplier of the list, or you may have to conduct a pretest to arrive at a realistic estimate (that is, mail a packet to each member of a small representative group from the sample to determine the rate of bad returns). Ideally, you will have conducted at least one pilot pretest of your questionnaire and methodology (see Chapter 3). A pilot test of the methods and questionnaire to be used in your final study can provide you with an estimate of the rate of bad returns while allowing you to assess the performance of the questionnaire.

There are two approaches you can take to compensate for bad addresses: You can decide not to pursue the bad addresses and simply include enough overage in the sample draw to compensate for the undeliverables, or you can try to track the correct addresses. Usually, no matter how good your tracking efforts, you will never find some respondents. You should also be aware that by simply replacing bad addresses with good ones (e.g., not tracking new information on the original sample), you may introduce a level of bias into your results, because you will be including only those respondents who are easy to reach or who are either residentially or occupationally less mobile. This can have major consequences, depending on the focus of the research.

The next element you need to consider in estimating sample size is the anticipated response rate, or the proportion of subjects from the sample population who will complete and return the questionnaire within the study time period. The proportion of respondents who do not participate compared with the number who could have is referred to as the *nonresponse rate*. Response rates for mail surveys can vary widely, depending on the accuracy of the sampled addresses, the rigor of the follow-up procedures, the quality of presentation of the study materials, and respondent incentive or interest in the study topic.

Another element in the success or failure of any survey, self-administered or mailed, is timing. If at all possible, you should avoid initiating your survey during the winter holiday season. Generally, postal volume increases at that time of year, and you do not want your survey to risk being delayed or lost in delivery because of the extra load being handled by the postal service at this time. Also, many households and businesses are inundated during the holidays with charity appeals, mail-order catalogs, and other "pulp" materials. Your survey runs a greater risk of being discarded or put aside during these peak periods. Finally, you do not want to conduct your survey at a time when individuals are already overloaded with preparations for holiday festivities. The summer months, when many people tend to go on vacation, can also be a deadly time for response rates, depending on the types of individuals being surveyed.

OTHER FACTORS AFFECTING RESPONSE RATES

Researchers have conducted mailing experiments to test hand-addressed envelopes versus envelopes with typed addresses, typed versus affixed labels, and affixed postage versus metered postage. Some of these treatments have been found to have positive but statistically nonsignificant effects on response rates, but special treatment of mailings does have beneficial effects. We have already discussed the accuracy of sampled addresses; we cover follow-up procedures and respondent motivation later in this chapter. Response rates for mail surveys can be 30% or lower when follow-up is minimal and the samples are composed of disinterested, unmotivated respondents. Conversely, when surveyors make repeated contact with respondents by mail and by telephone and a large portion of the respondents are interested and motivated, response rates of 70% or more can be achieved.

Components of the Field or Mailing Packet

The successful completion of self-administered surveys, especially mail surveys, requires good coordination and great attention to detail because of the numerous steps involved. The best way for the surveyor to impose organization on a self-administered study is to make a checklist of all the major steps involved. The best way for the surveyor to anticipate the steps that will be involved is first to make a checklist of the components of the group administration or mailing packet.

Group Administration Packet Checklist

✓ Sample: Access and means of selection?

✓ Schedule: Calendar of date/time/place

✓ Informed consent: If necessary, quantity?

✓ Cover letter: Print quantity?

✓ Questionnaire: Print quantity?

✓ Incentive: If used, quantity?

✓ Other handouts: If any, quantity?

✓ Means of retrieval: Collect/box/mail back?

Mailing Packet Checklist

✓ Sample labels/addresses: Quantity? Number of follow-ups?

✓ Outgoing mail envelopes: Quantity? Size of questionnaire? Additional materials? Number of follow-ups?

✓ Outgoing postage: Metered or stamped?

✓ Cover letter: Print quantity? Initial letter? Follow-up letter(s)?

✓ Questionnaire: Print quantity? Number of remailings?

✓ Incentive: If used, quantity?

✓ Other inserts: If any, quantity?

✓ Return mail envelopes: Postage-paid business reply/metered/stamps? Number of remailings?

Follow-Up Procedures

The surest way you can increase response rates is through follow-ups—that is, by recontacting potential respondents to remind them to complete the questionnaire and mail it back. Follow-ups can take the form of postcards, letters, telephone calls, or complete remailings. Some survey researchers use mailgrams or telegrams or overnight, registered, or certified mail to recontact potential respondents, draw their attention to the study, and stress the importance of each return. Minimally, you will want to send follow-up postcards or letters to either nonrespondents alone or the entire sample approximately 10 days after you post your initial mailing. These postcards or letters should remind respondents that they have been sent a questionnaire to fill out and return, restate the importance of their participation, and encourage them to take a few minutes to respond to the questionnaire now if they have not already done so. In this first follow-up, you should also provide respondents with the name and telephone number of someone on the project staff they can call (collect, if possible) if they have misplaced their questionnaires and want replacements sent. Figure 3.7 in Chapter 3 displays the text of the follow-up postcard we used in the Workplace Assault Study.

In your initial follow-up letter or postcard, you should indicate that you are aware of the possibility that the respondent has already completed and mailed the materials and apologize for any nuisance the follow-up mailing may cause. Sometimes, it is useful to offer the respondent an excuse for not responding, such as "We recognize how busy your schedule must be"; "Perhaps, like many of us do when we are busy, you have put the questionnaire to one side and forgotten it"; or "Perhaps someone else in your office/household has mistakenly thrown the questionnaire away." If you include a reason such as this last one, follow it with a reassurance that all the respondent needs to do is call and another packet will be sent. Of course, if you are working with a postcard, the text will have to be brief; probably all you will be able to accomplish will be to ask the respondent to complete the questionnaire and send it back.

Another option for getting questionnaires to and from some respondents is transmission by fax machine. However, if the subject matter of the survey is such that completed questionnaires will reveal confidential material about respondents, you should not suggest that respondents use this method to return their questionnaires unless you are able to guarantee that no one outside the project team could possibly see the material.

Depending on the nature and confidentiality of your study, you will probably find it useful to assign a unique identification number to each subject in the sample population prior to mailing. This number should be printed somewhere on the questionnaire itself (the back or the last page is least obtrusive) or on the return mail envelope. If you are explicit about the measures you are taking to ensure confidentiality in the cover letter you send with the questionnaire, most respondents will not react negatively to seeing identification numbers on their materials. There are always the few exceptions, however; some respondents will scratch out or tear off their identification numbers.

There are two major reasons you should assign identification numbers before mailing. First, the numbers will enable you to keep track of who has responded by logging the returns against a master sample list of the individuals to whom you sent the mailing. Knowing who has not responded will allow you to limit your follow-up efforts to only that group of individuals rather than the entire sample. In a large study, this will help you to realize significant savings in the time and cost involved in conducting follow-ups. Second, by identifying the sample you can sometimes create a profile of the nonresponding group so that you may venture an estimate of how alike or different the respondents and nonrespondents are. Clearly, the more alike they are, the better your data will represent the sampled population.

TYPE, NUMBER, AND TIMING OF FOLLOW-UPS

You need to consider several issues when planning follow-ups for your survey: the types of follow-ups, the number to be conducted, and how frequently or at what critical times you will administer them. Typically, you should base these decisions on the resources available to you and the amount of time you have allotted for your study.

You will find that producing sample status reports, as discussed earlier, will be invaluable in helping you decide what follow-up measures you need to take. For example, if the sample status report shows that after the first follow-up you have received 80% of your expected returns, you may decide to conduct only one more follow-up. If you are collecting data in a group setting and your "completes" are coming in at a faster rate than expected, you may need to alter your sampling interval to collect respondents at a slower rate, or you may want to shorten the period of time during which you collect data. Conversely, if after your first follow-up you have only received 20% of your expected returns, you may decide to conduct more intensive follow-ups, such as telephone calls and priority mailings, sooner than originally anticipated. If your sample status reports show a particularly high rate of bad addresses—that is, the number of undeliverables is so high you are unlikely to obtain the minimally desired number of returns—you may want to pursue the possibility of pulling another sample. In a group administration, if the number of completes is lower than anticipated, you may shorten the sampling interval, add more days to the administration period, or add more sites of administration.

Mailed follow-ups require additional printing, postage, envelopes, and labor. You can conduct telephone follow-ups only if you have valid telephone numbers for your respondents, and such follow-ups require considerable labor and the space and equipment to conduct the telephone calls, which may involve toll or long-distance charges aside from the monthly cost of the telephone. Depending on the type of sample you are seeking, survey staff may need to make numerous calls to contact each respondent (this is particularly true with elite samples, such as doctors, public figures, and corporate executives).

As we have noted, conducting follow-ups is the best means of increasing response rate. At minimum, you will want to send a postcard reminder to each person in your sample who has not returned a completed questionnaire. Typically, this postcard is sent 10 days to 2 weeks after the initial mailing date, with subsequent follow-ups made at 2-week or longer intervals.

If you have the time and resources to conduct several follow-ups of various types, it is often best to begin with the least expensive method first—postcard or letter—and use more expensive methods later, such as complete remailing of the packet, priority mailings (e.g., registered or certified letters, mailgrams), and telephone calls. If you have been able to keep a log of your sample returns and can identify who has not responded, you will be using the more expensive methods on increasingly smaller sample sizes. Although this is the most economical approach, you will find that you do not always have the luxury of time to consider this.

The greatest efficiency for follow-ups seems to peak at about three or four. Obviously, if time and money are of no consequence, you may make as many attempts as you wish. There does come a point, however, at which it makes no sense and is in fact no longer relevant to push for returns. This is a highly individual decision. If response has been particularly poor on a study, some researchers will continue to make follow-up attempts using every resource available. Remember, the credibility of the study rests in large part on the number of sampled individuals you have successfully represented.

When surveyors employ telephone calls as a follow-up method, it is not uncommon for them to use the calls as a means of gathering the data rather than simply to ask respondents to mail in their questionnaires. This assumes that the individuals making the calls are familiar with telephone interviewing and with the questionnaire and are capable of collecting the data in a competent manner. A telephone interview is only possible when the questionnaire is relatively brief and does not require the respondent to have access to other information, such as files or records, to answer the questions. In studies where self-administration is the only desirable method due to sensitivity of the topic or the perceived honesty of respondents, surveyors cannot use follow-up telephone calls to collect the data.

If you do collect some of your data using the telephone, it is wise to indicate in the data set which questionnaires were self-administered and which were completed through telephone interviews. In survey jargon, this is known as using *mixed methodologies*. It has been established that the various modes of survey administration—in-person interview, telephone interview, self-administered—have different effects on respondents and hence on the data. If you have used mixed methodologies, you should compare the results found with each of the modes of administration when you analyze your data to ensure that the distribution of answers across questions is not dramatically different. If you find gross differences, you may decide to report the information from the two methods separately or combine the two but report your findings with a caveat about possible unreliability of the data, or you may decide not to use the data obtained by a method different from that used to collect the majority.

If you are using self-administered questionnaires in a group setting, there is often little you can do to follow up on those individuals who were not present at the time of administration. If your study is being conducted in a relatively structured setting, however, such as a classroom, clinic, or workplace, you may be able to keep track of all individuals who were not in attendance at the time of administration. In such a case, you may be able to approach these individuals either at another visit or through other persons (e.g., teachers, nurses, or supervisors) who have contact with them, or you may be able to reach them by telephone. In deciding whether to make such follow-up contacts, you should consider whether there is a risk of "contaminating" the data, in that the nonrespondents may have had the opportunity to discuss the contents of the survey with those who were present at the time of administration. This may lead them to respond to the questionnaire differently than they would have if they had answered without prior knowledge.

In situations where you have third parties deliver self-administered questionnaires to the sampled individuals (such as schoolchildren taking questionnaires home for their parents to complete), you can have the same couriers (in this case, the students) take reminders to the respondents.

CONTENT OF THE FOLLOW-UP REMINDER

The wording of your first follow-up communication should be similar to that in the initial cover letter sent with the first mailing. If you are using a postcard, it could be worded as simply as this:

> A few weeks ago you received a questionnaire from [name of sponsor/researcher/organization] asking for your participation in a very important study about [topic]. To date we have not received your response. It is very important that we be able to include your opinions in our study. If you have already responded, thank you for your help and excuse this card. If you have not responded, won't you please take a minute now to do so? If you require additional information, please call [contact person and telephone number] collect. Again, thank you.

If you are using a letter, you can expand on the importance of the study and its purpose or use. Emphasize how important the respondent is to the success of your study and mention that he or she is one of a select few who have been picked to represent hundreds or thousands of others, depending on the universe from which the sample was drawn. Reinforce that the data are confidential and that the individual will not be identified in any way. If you have the endorsement or sponsorship of an individual or organization known to the respondent, remind the respondent about that. Finally, provide a name and telephone number where the individual may call for more information or to have another packet sent.

If you are using the telephone to make follow-up contacts, you need to select carefully the individuals who will make the calls. Callers should have pleasant, friendly voices, and, unless you are dealing with a non-English-speaking population, they should have speaking patterns similar to those of the people in your sample. If reminder calls are made by individuals with heavy accents, respondents may become frustrated trying to understand them and possibly will become alienated from your study.

All callers should work from a written script that is similar in content to the follow-up letter. Callers should identify themselves, their affiliation, and the purpose of the call. Again, the importance of the study and the respondent's participation should be the focus. The script should also contain all the information the caller will need to answer any questions a respondent might have. Although each caller will develop an individual style for effectiveness, the script will help to prevent callers from creating dialogue on the spot or giving information to respondents that may be misleading or untrue. In some cases, it may be necessary for a higher-level supervisor or even the researcher to speak on the telephone with a reluctant respondent.

If you decide to use the telephone to gather data from the individuals you successfully contact, you should pretest the questionnaire a few times over the telephone to make sure that it will adapt well to telephone administration. Self-administered questionnaires often include some kinds of questions that do not lend themselves well to telephone interviewing and may need to be modified in some way. This is another reason you should keep track of which interviews were conducted via telephone versus self-administration:

Changing the format of questions can produce dramatically different results.

If you are conducting multiple follow-ups, you will find it profitable to determine the response rate after you try each method. For example, if your first follow-up is a postcard, note how many returns come in after you send the card and before you use the next method. If the next method is a remailing of all the study materials, you might mark the questionnaires that go out in that mailing in some way so that when they are returned you can differentiate between returns from the first mailing and returns from the second. If you keep track of the effects of each procedure, the next time you conduct a mail survey you will be better able to judge how many and which follow-ups will give the best return for the investment. It is possible you will even find this information useful later in your study. If your goal is to get as many returns as is humanly possible, you may want to evaluate which methods worked best with your sample population and try them again.

Whether you use postcards, letters, or telephone calls, follow-up attempts are extremely important to the overall success of any study. Because they are so important, you should not treat these procedures casually. Method of delivery, content, and quality of presentation all leave an impression on the potential respondent. You will witness the rewards for your efforts in the level of response you receive.

Follow-Up Procedure Guidelines

- Ten days after the original mailing, send the first follow-up.

- Follow-ups can take the form of postcards, letters, or telephone calls.

- Use a mailgram or telegram or overnight, registered, or certified mail to call more attention to the survey mailing.

- Consider sending and/or receiving questionnaires via fax machine.

- Stress the importance of response and the purpose of the study in all follow-up messages.

- Include in the text of a follow-up letter or postcard the name and telephone number of a survey staff member the respondent can contact for assistance.

- Conduct additional follow-ups every 10 days.

- Keep track of the rate of return for each follow-up method used.

SAMPLE TRACKING

There are two basic types of mailing addresses: residential and commercial. In designing your study, you will have decided whether the sample target is a particular individual, an address, or a position. In other words, do you want Jane Doe at 111 Main Street, or is any adult living at 111 Main Street appropriate? Do you want John Smith, employee benefits manager for Company XYZ, or whoever is filling the position of employee benefits manager at XYZ? When the latter is the case, if a mailed packet is returned because the specific individual named is no longer there, you do not need to track the address; you can simply change the name or make the addressee noncommittal, such as "Resident" or "Employee Benefits Manager." Ideally, you will have set the address file up this way at the onset of the work, so that something like this only rarely becomes an issue.

When you are mailing to specific individuals, tracking becomes essential. In the case of bad addresses or unknown addressees, the U.S. Postal Service will not automatically notify you of such outcomes. If an addressee has moved and the mail forwarding order is active, the packet will automatically be sent to the new address, and you will not be notified about the updated address (forwarding orders are active for only one year). If a packet is undeliverable due to a bad address, no such person, or other condition, it often remains in a "dead letter" bin at the post office without your knowledge.

You would be wise to use a rubber stamp to mark each outgoing mailing packet "RETURN SERVICE REQUESTED" or, if you use an envelope-addressing program, to incorporate this wording into the address. The U.S. Postal Service will charge you 50¢ for each address correction it provides, but by using this procedure you will retain better control of the sample.

Bad addresses can also occur through human error. If an envelope is returned with a notation of "no such address," "no such number," or "no such street," you may be able to clear up the problem with some common sense and a quick check of a local street guide. It could be that the street name was misspelled, that the street name needs a directional specification (i.e., *North, South, East,* or *West*), or that the zip code is wrong. When you receive information about changes in addresses, you should remail the packets to the correct addresses and make sure the appropriate changes are also made in the sample files for future follow-up contacts.

If you do not receive new addresses for some respondents through the postal service or you cannot easily correct other bad addresses, you may want to try to track the missing respondents in a number of different ways if time and your budget allow. The first place you should go when looking for address updates is the sample supplier. It is possible that the supplier has new addresses or address corrections for sampled respondents that have not yet been changed in the main data file.

Typically, however, even if the supplier is able to provide some corrections, some address problems will still be unresolved. Business addresses are typically easier to track than those for individuals. If you need an address for a local business, you might find it simply by looking in the telephone directory, checking both residential and classified listings. The local telephone company's directory information line may be another resource, especially if the business you are trying to find has recently moved. Reverse directories—that is, telephone directories in which listings are arranged by street addresses and by telephone numbers instead of by the names of people and businesses (also called cross-reference or crisscross directories)—are also useful for tracking. Several major companies publish such directories; you may find them in your public library or at your local telephone company headquarters.

As the geographic area of your sample gets wider, the number of resources you might need to track sample addresses gets more complex. Typically, most institutions maintain only local directories. However, it is not unusual for large public libraries to have telephone directories available for many major metropolitan areas. In addition, your local telephone company headquarters may maintain a reference library of all the telephone directories produced by the parent company. If you have a large number of addresses to be checked, you may decide it is worthwhile to pay a directory publishing company to run the checks for you against the company's computer database. Many marketing companies and directory publishers maintain address files for the majority of mailing addresses in the United States and often can provide certain types of samples. They can produce mailing labels, and some will fold, stuff, seal, and post your mailing for you for a price.

The accessibility of information about particular individuals varies widely across the United States. Some states' departments of motor vehicles will allow searches of driver's license information, usually for a fee. Other states, like California, require permission from the individual license holder before the DMV can release any information. In any case, if you have the name, date of birth, and last known address of the individual you are tracking, that can help narrow down the possibilities.

You may also be able to get some help in finding respondents from local public utilities, such as the gas, water, and electricity companies. Regulations governing who can obtain this type of information vary considerably from area to area, however. Public utilities and other resources in large metropolitan areas are less likely to provide information on individuals than are those located in less populated areas.

Sample Tracking Procedure Guidelines

- Check for typographical and/or clerical errors in addresses.

- Stamp outgoing envelopes "RETURN SERVICE REQUESTED" and correct the address file based on corrected returns.

- Check with the sample provider for address updates, if applicable.

- Check telephone directories, telephone directory information, and reverse directories.

- Check with local utility companies and/or the state's department of motor vehicles.

- Remail packets to all corrected addresses.

Processing Returns

Having a plan for processing the returned questionnaires is as important as collecting the data. By *processing*, we mean applying particular methods to record the receipt of the completed questionnaires and to convert the data from these instruments into numeric results ready for analysis. In the following discussion, we assume that the returns will be entered into a computer file and read into some software that you can use to compile the results and, hopefully, calculate at least basic statistics on the findings. Some self-administered surveys are processed and analyzed by hand rather than on computers, but most of the processing procedures we discuss in this section pertain mainly to computer tabulation.

SAMPLE STATUS REPORTS

Earlier, we discussed the merits of maintaining a sample log or roster, either in paper-and-pencil form or computerized, on which you can check in your returns. Ideally, for each questionnaire this log should reflect the identification number assigned to the respondent; the number and types of follow-ups; procedures used to track the respondent, if any; corrections to the mailing file, if any; and the date the completed questionnaire was received. In organizations that routinely conduct surveys, the next item in the log might be the date when the questionnaire is turned over to data reduction. The ideal sample log is one that allows you to find out the location and status of any given questionnaire upon request.

DATABASE MANAGEMENT

Database management includes data entry, data cleaning, and various kinds of data processing. Prior to actual data entry, it is sometimes necessary to edit the completed questionnaires, code any open-ended material, provide codes for missing data, and eliminate incorrect responses. Many of the software programs available for creating machine-readable files will allow you to assign codes for missing data automatically and thus eliminate or greatly reduce incorrect responses. In some organizations, data may still be keypunched onto 80-column cards and read into computers, but in most instances, the data are entered directly onto the hard drive or onto a diskette using one of the many pro-grams available. Data can be entered into a spreadsheet pro-gram, such as Excel, directly from the questionnaire or from a codebook. They can also be entered into a statistical pro-gram, such as SAS or SPSS. The questionnaire can be scanned and then transferred into a program that will allow the data file to be created as the data are collected, such as in an online survey.

Returned questionnaires should not go to data entry without prior editing. Respondents may have skipped ques-tions or entire sections of the questionnaire, or they may have recorded several answers where they have been asked for only one. Some respondents may have answered ques-tions that they should have skipped based on their answers to some prior questions. Other respondents may have felt that the answer categories given were insufficient and decided to write in their own alternative answers. Some respondents will have handwriting that is barely legible. The ways individuals can find for not following instructions (no matter how straightforward the instructions or how simple the questions) are as varied and numerous as are the differ-ences between and among people. For all these reasons, you should always plan to have someone edit each completed questionnaire—that is, look it over for errors and other prob-lems—prior to data entry.

How the inconsistencies and inaccuracies found during the editing process are handled is up to the discretion of the researcher. If an answer is missing but the researcher feels the respondent's intended response is obvious, he or she may allow the editor to make the necessary correction. In some cases, researchers might have staff members call respondents (when their telephone numbers are available) to clarify responses or to obtain responses the respondents neglected to fill in on the questionnaire. In other cases, researchers might choose to code for "no response" where problematic answers appear. In any case, you need to develop a plan whereby inconsistent, incorrect, or missing data are either assigned numeric values or skipped altogether.

Who handles the editing varies. In some survey houses, the questionnaires are edited by field clerks in an area that specializes in the collection of data. In other places, the questionnaires are edited as part of the coding process. During coding, written answers are converted into numeric codes according to an established coding scheme or plan known as a *codebook*. A coding clerk may edit and code the instrument in one step. In some studies, the editing, coding, and data entry are performed concomitantly. We do not recommend this system, however; we believe it places too great a burden on the individual and invites error. If you are going to have the same person perform all tasks, it would be better if you have editing and coding done in one step and the data entry done separately. (For more in-depth discussion of the processing of data, see **How to Manage, Analyze, and Interpret Survey Data**, Volume 9 in this series, as well as Bourque and Clark's *Processing Data*, which is included in the "Suggested Readings" section at the end of this book.)

Estimating Costs

Typically, you will be required to develop an estimate of the costs of conducting your mail or other self-administered survey prior to the time you actually begin to incur expenses. The first decision you must make before you can estimate costs concerns sample size. Specifically, you will need to estimate how many initial mailings you anticipate, how many completed returns you expect, and the costs for address corrections (if you plan to use this option). In the following pages, we first address the expenses unique to mail surveys and then examine the costs associated with self-administered surveys that are distributed by means other than mail. Finally, we address the costs that occur with both methods.

There are two types of costs: out-of-pocket expenses and constant costs, or costs for labor that is expended whether or not the study is conducted. Out-of-pocket expenses are those that you must pay—that is, expenses for items not routinely paid for by your organization. Such costs might include postage, printing, envelopes, incentives, and any labor required for tasks that are not covered by employees who are already paid for. An example of an out-of-pocket cost for labor is the use of a mailing company to fold, stuff, and affix labels and postage to your mailing.

A word of caution: The expenditures itemized in the following pages reflect approximate costs as of September 2002. Postal rates and other costs are subject to change; some costs will vary considerably from region to region. Labor charges that are inherent in certain tasks will vary by location, and such charges, like postal rates, tend to undergo frequent increases. Other overhead costs and markups will vary depending on the expense of doing business in different areas. Finally, you may be able to get lower prices on stock materials, such as envelopes and paper, than are shown here, depending on how much you buy—generally, costs go down as volume increases. The dollar amounts presented here are meant as guidelines only—you should find out the appropriate costs for the items you need in your own market area.

OUTGOING POSTAGE

For a mailed study, you will need a postal scale that can accurately weigh ounces, so you can estimate your postage expense. Postal scales are commonly found in most office settings. Assemble a packet that mimics what you plan to send; for example, include an outgoing mail envelope, a return mail envelope, a sheet of paper to represent the cover letter, pages to represent the questionnaire (use the number of pages you anticipate you will have in the final version, but remember that if you print the questionnaire on a slightly heavier paper stock to avoid print bleed-through, the overall weight of the real instrument may end up being significantly heavier than the mock-up you tested), the incentive (if you plan to use one), and any other materials you plan to include in this mailing. Weigh all of these materials together on the scale to find out the total weight of the outgoing packet.

Using the same mock-up packet, remove the page representing the cover letter, the outgoing envelope, the incentive, and any materials other than the return mail envelope and questionnaire and/or any other materials to be sent back by the respondent. Weigh what is left to find out the weight in ounces of the return mail packet. (You will need this information to figure out the amount of postage required to return the packet to you. We discuss the cost of providing return mail postage below.)

Always send materials at the first-class postage rate. If you use second-, third-, or fourth-class or other bulk-rate postage, you send the message that the study and the respondent are not important to you. As of September 2002, the rate for outgoing first-class postage was 37¢ for the first ounce and 23¢ for each additional ounce or fraction of an ounce. The U.S. Postal Service offers discounts off this rate for large mailings that are presorted by zip code. To qualify for this discount, you must have a minimum number of pieces outgoing to each zip code in your mailing. If you can meet the requirements, the discount rate is 35¢ per ounce. The postal service also offers other cost breaks for mailings that use "ZIP+4" or bar codes. You would be wise to inquire at your local post office about rates and requirements before you make a cost estimate and set up your sample specifications.

When preparing your cost estimate, you also need to include the cost of postage to conduct follow-ups, if any. The cost of mailing a postcard is currently 23¢, and the U.S. Postal Service sells single postage-paid postcards for 25¢. Again, the postal service offers discounts for mailings that are presorted using ZIP+4 or bar codes. If you are planning to send letters as reminders, you should assume that each will be an ounce (i.e., will cost 37¢ to mail). You can also buy personalized, stamped no. 10 envelopes from the U.S. Postal Service. Whether or not you decide to use such stamped envelopes will depend on the resources you have available. If you work in a setting where there is a clerk who can put your mailings through a postage meter, you may not need to buy prestamped envelopes. Similarly, if you can get a better volume discount on the printing of personalized envelopes or if such envelopes are freely available to you at your place of work, it makes no monetary sense for you to purchase prestamped envelopes.

Finally, you should remember that if you intend to remail the entire study packet to respondents as a follow-up at some point, you should include in your cost estimate the postage the remailing will require; the cost per piece will be the same as in your original mailing.

INCOMING POSTAGE

You must include a self-addressed, postage-paid envelope with the mailing for the respondent to use in returning the questionnaire. You have two options for providing return mail postage: You can affix sufficient postage in the form of stamps to preaddressed return envelopes, or you can open a business reply mail (BRM) account with your post office and use preprinted, postage-paid BRM envelopes. Affixing postage can be a waste of money in that not all respondents will complete and return the questionnaire, so you will have spent the money for postage without receiving a return. The postage-paid BRM option costs more than the regular per ounce postal rate, because when you open a BRM account you must pay a 12-month permit fee of $150.00, plus you pay a surcharge for handling. If your mailing is large enough, however, you will find that using BRM will be much more economical than providing postage in the mailing.

There are two surcharge rates for BRM handling. If your expected return is fewer than 600 pieces, your post office will require a deposit of $475.00 to open an account for handling returns, and the additional charge per piece over and above the postage will be 60¢ with a basic permit. As questionnaires are returned, the postal charges are subtracted from the initial deposit of $475 until that money is exhausted. If your expected return is more than 600 pieces, you should contact your local post office to determine your eligibility to use BRM and how much it will cost. Higher-volume BRM permits can qualify for lower-per-piece return rates.

OTHER DELIVERY OPTIONS

The U.S. Postal Service offers several kinds of special handling that you might consider using: return receipt requested at the time of mailing, showing who signed for the packet and on what date, at $1.75 per piece; registered mail at $7.50; Express Mail, next-day delivery, at $13.65; or certified mail at $2.30 (again, these were the prices as of September 2002). You might also consider having your packets delivered by Federal Express, United Parcel Service, or another private courier service. Although these options may be more expensive than first-class U.S. mail, they will draw attention to your study and communicate its importance to your respondents. Although budgetary constraints are always a consideration, you may decide that paying for a method of delivery that enhances the quality of the presentation of the study materials is more important than saving a few dollars, especially if saving money on delivery might contribute to your getting a response rate so low that it makes the study unusable. Address correction service will cost 70¢ per piece for manual notice and 20¢ for each electronic return. You will not be able to anticipate which of your returns will be corrected manually and which will be handled electronically, as that depends on the post office returning the mail, so you should estimate your anticipated returns at the higher rate.

PRINTED AND STOCK MATERIALS

The next budget item for consideration is the cost of printed materials for the study. You may already have access to some of these items, such as outgoing envelopes, and so may not need to purchase them; others you will need to buy.

It is assumed that your materials for printing will be camera-ready. That is, you will have typed or word processed the final products as they will appear in print. Your printing contractor will either photograph the originals and create negatives for printing or use a duplicating process such as photocopying. The quality of duplication today is such that you can barely tell the difference between a printed page and a page generated by a high-quality photocopying machine.

If your mailing is not bulky, you may be able to use no. 11 (4 1/2-by-10 1/2-inch) envelopes for your outgoing packets and no. 10 (4 1/2-by-91/2-inch) envelopes for returns of the completed questionnaires. By "not bulky," we mean that your questionnaire is brief (no more than one 11-by-17-inch page folded and printed front and back, resulting in four printed sides), your cover letter is one page, you use a no. 10 reply envelope, and that there are no additional inserts to the mailing. The cost for 500 nonpersonalized no. 11 envelopes is approximately $27.00; for 500 no. 10s, about $16.00.

For larger mailings, you will need to use flats, or larger envelopes. Not only can you put thicker materials into these envelopes, you do not have to prefold all the pages before stuffing them into the envelopes. Heavy-duty 10-by-13-inch self-sealing, white first-class envelopes cost approximately $142.00 per 500. You will need to include in your mailing packets the same type of envelopes for returning the questionnaires, but they will be smaller (9-by-12-inch) envelopes; these cost about the same as the slightly larger size.

The outgoing envelopes should have your project name, organization name, and address imprinted in the upper left-hand corner or the sender section. The incoming envelopes must have your business address in the addressee section in the middle of the front; you may also want to repeat your address in the upper left-hand corner or the sender section of these envelopes. If the return address you are using receives a fairly high volume of mail on a regular basis, you will want to identify your project on the face of the incoming envelopes, either on the lower left-hand side or as a line in the addressee section. This will help the mail sorter identify your packets and deliver them in a timely fashion. If you are using bar coding, you will also need to print this on the incoming envelopes.

In estimating project costs, you should allow approximately 4¢ per piece for imprinting addresses. It is possible that your printer will be able to bid the entire printing job, including the cost for imprinting the envelopes, at a rate lower than you would get if you were to have each printing job done separately. Again, when costing your study, remember to include the cost for additional follow-up mailing envelopes.

Other items that you will need to have printed are the cover letter and the questionnaire. Printing costs for 500 letters on 20-pound bond paper will be approximately $30.00. The total cost for 500 copies of a questionnaire printed on both sides of one piece of 11-by-17-inch paper and folded into a booklet (for a total of four questionnaire pages) will be about $125.00 (the cost per printed questionnaire page comes out to about 6.25¢). Remember that these costs will fluctuate from area to area due to varying labor and overhead costs, and they will also vary depending on the weight and type of paper used for printing and the means by which the questionnaires are bound. When you are having questionnaires printed on both sides of each page, it is better to use 60-pound paper to eliminate the possibility of print bleeding through to the other side, although the heavier paper does cost a bit more.

Always order more copies of all items from the printer than you think you will need. In other words, if you are mailing to 500 respondents, you should have 600 copies printed. You will need to have some extras on hand in case some of the printing is imperfect and to replace any that might get lost or damaged. Also, you can distribute extra copies to other members of the survey project staff so that they can become familiar with all the study materials, and you can store some copies in your archival file to document the study.

Before you release materials for printing, you will need to decide whether you will be making a second complete mailing to your sample. If you will, you should have the necessary materials for the second mailing printed at the same time as the rest, because it is more economical to have everything printed at one time (volume reduces cost per piece, plus do not have to pay two separate job-setup fees). Always allow sufficient time before your mailing date for the printing to be done. If you need to ask for rush printing because you are on an extremely tight schedule, your printer will charge extra. When estimating printing costs, remember to include the cost of printing follow-up letters and other materials you may use in addition to the questionnaire.

If you plan to use an incentive, the cost obviously will be dependent on the gift. You can purchase small key chains for about 25¢ each or retractable ballpoint pens for around 50¢ each, or you may elect to enclose a $1 bill in the mailing (if you do, make sure that you send new, clean bills). Estimate the most you would spend on an incentive and multiply that cost by the sample size to get a figure for your cost estimate. If you plan to include other materials in your mailing, you will need to add the costs for these into your budget.

PERSONNEL REQUIREMENTS

Material expenses are but one part of the costs of conducting survey studies; such studies also involve a considerable amount of labor. Mail surveys generally require more labor than do self-administered surveys distributed by means other than mail, simply because there are a great many tasks to be performed that require considerable coordination and management. Much of the labor needed to conduct mail studies is at the skilled clerical level, but you will want the person coordinating your project to have the following characteristics: creative, detail oriented, good at managing tasks and individuals, good at problem solving, resourceful, skilled in communicating with vendors and other employees, and skilled in logical thinking. It would also be advantageous if your project manager has some degree of experience with word processing and spreadsheet programs, because ultimately you will need at least one person with these skills to produce your camera-ready copy of the questionnaire and set up a computerized record-keeping system for sample tracking. It would also be very helpful if your project manager has prior experience in obtaining bids for supplies and printing.

These same characteristics are desirable in an individual who manages a self-administered survey study in which the questionnaires are not distributed by mail. It is this person's responsibility to coordinate the printing and gathering of materials necessary to conduct the administration; to get cooperation from the sites to be included; to set up the logistics of date, time, and availability of the desired population; to provide the trained individuals who will go to these sites to distribute and collect the questionnaires, if appropriate; and to oversee the processing of the completed questionnaires as they are returned.

You may decide to contract out the most labor-intensive aspects of your study: folding the study materials and stuffing them into the outgoing envelopes, affixing the address labels, opening up the returns as they come in, editing and coding the completed questionnaires, and entering the data into a computer file. Companies that provide mailing services—that is, they fold, stuff, label, and post materials for a fee—can be found nearly everywhere, as are data processing companies that will open the envelopes, edit and code the questionnaires according to your specifications, and then enter the data into a file for you.

If no tabulating experts or facilities are available within your organization, you can also pay most data processing companies to process your data, provide you with frequency distributions (the count and percentage of the number of responses to each answer category in a question), and cross-tabulate the data to your specifications. If you are able to have this work performed within your organization, you will need the services of one or more clerical workers, depending on the size of the study. These workers must be good with detail and able to work well with numbers. One or a few of the clerks, depending on the volume of work, should have some word processing and/or spreadsheet experience, and at least one should have 10-key experience for data entry.

For a nonmail self-administered study, you may need clerical-level help to carry out the survey administration. These individuals will go to each study location, distribute the questionnaires to be completed, and monitor the administration. Depending on the complexity of the study, these individuals may have to conduct on-the-spot sampling, make random respondent selections, and make oral presentations regarding the purpose of the study and its sponsorship. They should be able to answer questions about particular items in the questionnaire and about the study in general. You should select these individuals for their ability to interact with others and to present themselves with a sense of competence and authority.

Unfortunately, the effort required to conduct either a mail or nonmail self-administered study is not constant over the duration of the project. There are times of heavy labor intensity and then times during which little or no labor is required. It is best if the management personnel you will require for your project are already in place in your organization and can allocate time to running the study.

The clerical time required is not as much of a problem. If clerical personnel are not routinely available in your setting, you may be able to find part-time hourly workers through temporary personnel agencies. Colleges and universities are also rich sources of clerical help in the form of students looking for part-time work. The hourly wages typical for clerical workers vary widely depending on geographic location and the level of skills required. Clerks who will fold, stuff, and affix labels need not be as skilled as those who will edit, code, and use personal computers. Wages for these workers may be as low as $6.00 or as high as $20.00 per hour.

To determine the number of clerical hours necessary to complete your project, you can use the guidelines shown in

Table 5.1, which lists time estimates for the tasks involved in a mail survey using a questionnaire with four open-ended questions and the rest precoded—that is, one 11-by-17-inch sheet folded in half (four printed pages), a no. 11 outgoing envelope, a no. 10 incoming envelope, and a cover letter. The figures in the table are based on the assumption that the clerical personnel employed are familiar with some of their functions—for example, that data entry personnel are proficient on 10-key pads.

TABLE 5.1   Time Estimates for Mail Survey Tasks

Task	Time
Folding survey materials, stuffing into envelopes, affixing labels to envelopes	100 packets/hour
Postal metering	500/hour
Opening envelopes and logging returns	120 envelopes/hour
Editing a 4-page questionnaire	30 questionnaires/hour
Coding 4 questions	12 questionnaires/hour
Entering 4 pages/30 questions into a computer file	30 questionnaires/hour

If this survey were to be mailed to 500 individuals, we would budget for 5 hours to fold the materials, stuff them into the envelopes, and affix the mailing labels. If you will need to have someone put the envelopes through a postage meter, add another hour to the clerical time.

For the purposes of this exercise, assume a response rate of 80%, or 400 returned, completed questionnaires. Opening those 400 envelopes and checking in each one by identification number against the master roster or log would take approximately 4 hours; it would take 14 hours to edit the questionnaires, 34 hours to code them, and another 14 hours to enter them into the computer data file.

All told, the study in this example would require 72 hours of clerical time to ready the packets for mailing, meter them, log in the returns, edit and code the questionnaires, and enter them into a data file. In your own time estimates, you will want to inflate these figures to account for break time, lunch periods, and other occasional pauses. Although you can arrange for the editing, coding, and data entry tasks to be held and done together, so that the clerical functions are done all at one time, the logging in of returns must be done piecemeal; someone must log them in as they come in so that you can keep track of your sample and response rate and, if necessary, take corrective measures.

The budget displayed in Table 5.2 illustrates how to use the cost estimates we have presented in this chapter. The figures in the table represent what it would cost in 2002 to conduct the Workplace Assault Study, which we have used as an example throughout this book. The table also includes the actual return rates at different stages of the data collection process in that study (at the time the first edition of this volume went to press, only estimates were available for some of these numbers).

Although some of the wage rates shown in Table 5.2 may not be applicable to your situation, this budget should give you a general idea of the materials and personnel you need to conduct a mail survey. It also illustrates that you may be able to share or eliminate some project costs by working with other individuals or groups who hold a common interest in the research. Obviously, the more you are able to offset costs within your organization, the lower your out-of-pocket expenses.

A common error made by novice surveyors doing their first mail surveys is failing to plan for enough resources to cover additional follow-ups if they become necessary. Even though you may have conducted a reasonable pilot test of your procedures and sample, there is always the possibility (as we saw in the case of the union employees' sample discussed in Chapter 2) that your pilot-test returns will not accurately reflect the total population returns for reasons that are not obvious at the time of planning. You should always have a contingency plan for what you will do if completed returns fall significantly short of the necessary sample goal. It would be a terrible loss to go through all the work required to conduct a survey only to find out that you have insufficient numbers of returns to make use of the data.

TABLE 5.2   Example Study Budget

Item	$ Cost
Development of Project	
Writing proposal: 4 days @ $500/day (senior author's UCLA salary rate/outside consulting rate would double)	2,000.00
First draft of questionnaire and specifications: 2 days @ $500/day (senior author's UCLA salary rate)	1,000.00
Finalizing questionnaire: 8 hours @ $17.60 (project coordinator's hourly rate)	140.80
Establishing contacts and meeting with union personnel: 15 hours @ $17.60	264.00
Organizing and conducting focus groups: 24 hours @ $17.60/hour	422.40
Pretesting questionnaire: 8 hours @ $17.60/hour	140.80
Miscellaneous administrative tasks (arranging meetings, clerical, etc.): 4 hours @ $17.60	70.40
TOTAL DEVELOPMENT COSTS	4,038.40
Mailings	
Purchase and printing of 4 sets of mailing labels (labor contributed by Service Employees International Union [SEIU])	259.90
Purchase of envelopes for advance letter and first mailing of questionnaire	773.60

(continued)

Item	$ Cost
Advance Letter	
Duplication of 1,800 letters @ 6¢/letter	108.00
Postage for 1,800 letters @ 34¢/letter	612.00
Labor associated with mailing letters contributed by SEIU	
First Mailing of Questionnaire	
Duplication of 1,800 flyers @ 6¢/flyer	108.00
Duplication of 1,800 cover letters @ 6¢/letter	108.00
Duplication of 1,800 22-page questionnaires @ 5¢/page	1,980.00
Postage to mail first questionnaire to 1,744 SEIU members @ $1.03/packet (SEIU provided metering service and labor to mail each packet)	1,796.32
Postage for 1,744 respondents to mail back first questionnaire @ 80¢/questionnaire (stamps placed on each return envelope)	1,395.20
Collation of 1,744 mailing packets: 54 hours @ $17.60/hour	950.40
TOTAL COST OF MAILING OF FIRST QUESTIONNAIRE	8,091.42
COST PER QUESTIONNAIRE MAILED	4.64
COST PER QUESTIONNAIRE RETURNED ($n = 310$)	26.10
Postcards	
Purchase of 1,800 postcards @ 23¢/card	414.00

(continued)

Item	$ Cost
Labor to print postcards contributed by SEIU	
Labor to put labels on postcards: 4 hours @ $17.60/hour	70.40
TOTAL COST OF MAILING POSTCARDS	484.40
ADDITIONAL COST PER RESPONDENT	0.28
COST PER ADDITIONAL RESPONSE OBTAINED ($n = 256$)	1.89
COST PER TOTAL RESPONSE OBTAINED ([$8,091.42 + $484.40]/566)	15.15
Second Mailing of Questionnaire	
Duplication of 1,107 cover letters @ 4¢/letter	66.42
Duplication of 1,107 22-page questionnaires @ 5¢/page	1,217.70
Purchase of 15 boxes of 10-by-13-inch envelopes: 100 envelopes/box @ $28.60/box	429.00
Printing of 1,500 envelopes @ 4¢/envelope	60.00
Postage for 1,107 packets @ $1.03 per packet	1,140.21
Postage paid on only those returned by business reply mail: [$125.00 + ($375.00 − [$0.78 × 191 packets])]	351.00
Collation of 1,107 mailing packets: 36 hours @ $17.60/hour	626.00
TOTAL COST OF SECOND FULL MAILING	3,890.35

(continued)

Item	$ Cost
COST PER ADDITIONAL QUESTIONNAIRE OBTAINED ($n = 191$)	20.37
COST PER TOTAL RESPONSE OBTAINED ([\$8,091.42 + 484.40 + \$3,890.35]/757)	16.47
Telephone Follow-Up	
As of April 1995, 756 of the 1,696 workers in the eligible sample (44.5%) had returned questionnaires. Of the 1,763 persons originally selected, 19 were excluded because of incomplete mailing addresses, 50 were excluded because they no longer worked for Los Angeles County, 49 questionnaires were returned marked "return to sender," and 35 potential respondents refused to participate in the study. Telephone interviews were attempted with the remaining 935 nonrespondents. Had this study been originally designed as a telephone survey, development costs would be included in this section.	
Screening conducted with 272 persons who did not report assaults @ $10 per interview	3,536.00
Interviewing conducted with 91 persons who did report assaults @ $25 per interview	3,185.00
Travel: 575 miles @ $0.345 per mile	198.38
Coordination: 40 hours @ $17.60	704.00
TOTAL COST OF TELEPHONE INTERVIEWS	8,457.12

(continued)

Item	$ Cost
COST PER ADDITIONAL QUESTIONNAIRE OBTAINED	23.30
COST PER TOTAL RESPONSE OBTAINED ([$8,091.42 + $484.40 + $3,890.35 + $8,457.12]/1,120)	18.68
Preliminary Data Processing and Analysis	
Logging in 1,120 questionnaires: 12 hours @ $17.60/hour	211.00
Data entry: 280 hours @ $17.60 per hour	4,928.00
Data cleaning and preliminary data processing and analysis: 500 hours @ $17.60 per hour	8,800
TOTAL PRELIMINARY PROCESSING AND ANALYSIS	13,939
TOTAL COST OF SURVEY EXCLUDING FINAL ANALYSIS AND WRITING	34,862.29
Supervisory time (supervision of mailings, data entry, data processing, data analysis, and writing) contributed by senior author and not included in total costs	

Exercises

1. The officers of a large corporation are considering changing the kinds of health insurance plans made available to the corporation's managerial and professional employees. They want to find out the kind of health insurance plans that employees currently have, both through the company and through other sources, and the extent to which employees express interest in three new plans currently under discussion. Would a self-administered questionnaire be appropriate for this study? If so, which <u>type</u> of self-administered questionnaire would you recommend using?

   One-to-one self-administered questionnaire   .1

   Group-administered questionnaire 2

   Semisupervised questionnaire passed out
      in the workplace .3

   Questionnaire mailed to employees' homes . .4

   Questionnaire administered online 5

   Do not use a self-administered
      questionnaire 6

2. The Parent-Teacher Association (PTA) of an elementary school wants to find out the number of active PTA members who think it would be a good idea to hold a carnival to raise money for extra computer software for the school *and* would be willing to help organize the carnival. Would a self-administered questionnaire be appropriate for this study? If so, which <u>type</u> of self-administered questionnaire would you recommend using?

    One-to-one self-administered questionnaire   .1

    Group-administered questionnaire 2

    Semisupervised questionnaire passed out
        as people arrive at a PTA meeting 3

    Semisupervised questionnaire passed out
        as people leave a PTA meeting 4

    Questionnaire mailed to students' homes 5

    Questionnaire administered online 6

    Do not use a self-administered
        questionnaire 7

3. The members of a neighborhood association are aware that a number of elderly Russian immigrants have moved into their community. It is their observation that many of these people are afraid to come out of their apartments. They want to find out what they can do to help these new residents of the community. Would a self-administered questionnaire be appropriate for this study? If so, which <u>type</u> of self-administered questionnaire would you recommend using?

    One-to-one self-administered questionnaire   .1

    Group-administered questionnaire 2

    Semisupervised questionnaire distributed
        at community meetings 3

Questionnaire mailed to residents' homes . . .4

Questionnaire administered online 5

Do not use a self-administered questionnaire .6

4. The staff members of a dental clinic located in a university dental school want to find out how satisfied patients are with their services. They have a draft questionnaire that they need to test to see if it is complete and to find out whether patients can fill it out. Would a self-administered questionnaire be appropriate for this study? If so, which <u>type</u> of self-administered questionnaire would you recommend using?

One-to-one self-administered questionnaire .1

Group-administered questionnaire 2

Semisupervised questionnaire 3

Questionnaire mailed to patients' homes 4

Questionnaire administered online 5

Do not use a self-administered
  questionnaire 6

5. The managers of a factory that manufactures ball bearings have received a lot of complaints from employees about homeless persons in the area around the factory. The managers have not seen many homeless in the area. They want to find out whether the complaints are representative of the total population of workers in the factory or simply the opinions of a few "squeaky wheels." Would a self-administered questionnaire be appropriate for this study? If so, which <u>type</u> of self-administered questionnaire would you recommend using?

One-to-one self-administered questionnaire .1

Group-administered questionnaire 2

Semisupervised questionnaire passed out
as workers punch in for work 3

Semisupervised questionnaire passed out
as workers punch out from work 4

Questionnaire mailed to workers' homes 5

Questionnaire administered online 6

Do not use a self-administered
questionnaire 7

6. The board of a regional symphony orchestra has
received a grant of $20,000 from the county govern-
ment to conduct a study to find out whether county
residents know about the symphony, whether they
have ever attended a concert, and the kinds of music
they prefer. Would a self-administered questionnaire
be appropriate for this study? If so, which <u>type</u> of self-
administered questionnaire would you recommend
using?

One-to-one self-administered questionnaire .1

Questionnaire administered at various group
meetings 2

Semisupervised questionnaire passed out
as people arrive at various
community meetings 3

Semisupervised questionnaire passed out
as people leave various
community meetings 4

Questionnaire mailed to a sample
of 500 county residential addresses 5

Questionnaire administered online 6

Do not use a self-administered
questionnaire 7

7. A questionnaire contains the following two questions:

    1. What are the three most important problems in your community today?

    _____

    _____

    _____

    2. People consider different things to be problems in their community. A list of 10 things that some people consider problems follows. Please rank order the list from 1 to 10, where 1 represents the problem you consider most important in your community and 10 represents the problem you consider least important in your community.

Problem	Rank Order
Street cleaning	_____
Corrupt officials	_____
Burglary and other crimes	_____
Mail delivery	_____
Telephone service	_____
Garbage and trash pickup	_____
Inadequate libraries	_____
Lack of up-to-date fire equipment	_____
Low water pressure	_____
Public schools	_____
Other	_____

SPECIFY: _____

Would a self-administered questionnaire be appropriate for this study? If so, which <u>type</u> of self-administered questionnaire would you recommend using?

One-to-one self-administered questionnaire   .1

Questionnaire administered at various group
   meetings 2

Semisupervised questionnaire passed out
   as people arrive at various
   community meetings 3

Semisupervised questionnaire passed out
   as people leave various
   community meetings 4

Questionnaire mailed to county residents'
   homes 5

Questionnaire administered online 6

Do not use a self-administered
   questionnaire 7

8. A study to be administered to high school juniors includes the following questions:

   1. Please give me the names of your five closest friends.

      _____

      _____

      _____

      _____

      _____

   2. For *each* person you named in Question 1, please tell whether that person is a male or female, how old, and whether s/he goes to this school.

PERSON   SEX   AGE   SAME SCHOOL?

_____

_____

_____

_____

_____

3. Have any of these five people ever done anything illegal, like drink or take drugs or steal something?

   No . . . . . . SKIP TO Q4 . . 1

   Yes . . . . . .ANSWER A . . 2

   A. Which of these five people have done something illegal?

   _____

   B. What did s/he do?

   _____

Would a self-administered questionnaire be appropriate for this study? If so, which <u>type</u> of self-administered questionnaire would you recommend using?

   One-to-one self-administered questionnaire .1

   Questionnaire administered in classrooms . . .2

   Semisupervised questionnaire passed out
      as students come to school 3

   Semisupervised questionnaire passed out
      as students leave school 4

   Questionnaire mailed to students' homes 5

   Do not use a self-administered
      questionnaire 6

9. Identify whether or not a mail questionnaire would be a reasonable way to collect data in each of the following situations.

   a. The city council wants to find out whether members of the Chamber of Commerce think a new parking structure should be built in the downtown area and the extent to which members would be willing to vote to pay higher taxes to construct such a structure.

   b. The school board wants to find out why the number of high school dropouts has increased over the past 5 years.

   c. Managers at a health insurance company want to find out how many childhood immunizations the company's members have had and when they had them.

   d. The officers of a college sorority want to find out the current employment status of the sorority's alumni.

   e. A local grocery store manager has recently placed an order for brown eggs because they were available at a substantially lower price than white eggs. Shortly after placing the order, the manager reads an article in the local newspaper that suggests county residents are not likely to buy brown eggs. The manager becomes concerned that the store will not be able to sell the brown eggs.

10. Identify why the following questions would or would not work well in a self-administered questionnaire.

   a. How much water do you drink every day?

1 ounce 1

2 ounces 2

3 ounces 3

4 ounces 4

5 ounces 5

6 ounces 6

7 ounces 7

8 ounces 8

9 ounces 9

10 ounces 10

11 ounces 11

12 ounces 12

13 ounces 13

14 ounces 14

b. Please describe all the jobs you have had for pay since you were 16 years old.

_____

_____

_____

c. How many times have you been hospitalized overnight?

Never . . . . .GO TO Q53 1

Once . . . . .GO TO Q40 2

Twice . . . . .GO TO Q27 3

Three or more times . .CONTINUE 4

d. Do you rent or own your place of residence?

Own 1

Rent 2

Other 3

SPECIFY: _____

e. What is your current marital status? Are you:

Married 1

Divorced 2

Separated 3

Widowed, or 4

Have you never been married? 5

f. How often do you see or hear from your children
or grandchildren?

_____

_____

_____

g. When do you watch the most TV? Would you say:

Monday 1

Tuesday 2

Wednesday 3

Thursday 4

Friday 5

Saturday, or 6

Sunday 7

    h. Have you ever been audited by the IRS?

        Yes 1

        No 2

11. The State Department of Parks and Recreation wants to find out how residents of the state spend their leisure time. What steps should the department take in developing a questionnaire to survey residents?

12. Would the following set of questions make a good self-administered questionnaire? Why or why not?

    1. How often do you vote? Would you say:

        Every election, or 1

        Something else? 2

        SPECIFY: _____

    2. Do you drink milk every day?

        Yes 1

        No 2

    3. What is your highest degree?

        No degree 1

        High school diploma . . . 2

        College degree 3

        Postcollege degree 4

        Something else 5

        SPECIFY: _____

4. Do you usually vote:

Republican 1

Democrat, or 2

Something else? 3

5. Are you on a special diet?

Yes 1

No 2

6. Are you registered to vote?

Yes 1

No 2

7. How many years of schooling have you completed and received credit for?

Less than 8 years 1

9-11 years 2

12 years 3

More than 12 years 4

13. Two companies are considering starting a car pool program. Management has developed the following questionnaire. What kinds of instructions are needed, and where would you put them?

1. How did you get to work yesterday? Did you:

Drive alone in a car 1

Drive in a car pool 2

Take the bus 3

Ride a motorcycle 4

Ride a bicycle 5

Walk, or 6

Something else? 7

SPECIFY: _____

2. Was yesterday a typical day for you? Is that the way you usually get to work?

Yes . . . . . . SKIP TO Q3 . .1

No . . . . . . .ANSWER A . . .2

    A. How do you usually get to work?

        Drive alone in a car .1

        Drive in a car pool . .2

        Take the bus 3

        Ride a motorcycle . .4

        Ride a bicycle 5

        Walk 6

        Something else 7

        SPECIFY: _____

3. Have you ever used the bus or other public transportation to get to work?

Yes, use public transportation now 1

Yes, used public transportation in the past . . .2

No, have never used public transportation . . .3

4. Have you ever considered using public transportation to get to work?

Yes, and currently use it 1

Yes, but decided it was too expensive 2

Yes, but decided it was too inconvenient 3

Yes, but decided against it for some
    other reason 4

SPECIFY: _____

No, never considered using it 5

5. Have you ever used car pools to get to work?

Yes, use a car pool now 1

Yes, used a car pool in the past 2

No, have never used a car pool 3

6. Have you ever considered using a car pool to get to work?

Yes, and currently use it 1

Yes, but decided it was too expensive 2

Yes, but decided it was too inconvenient 3

Yes, but decided against it for some
    other reason 4

SPECIFY: _____

No, never considered using it 5

7. If the company started a car pool program, would you be interested in using it?

Yes 1

No 2

8. Which of the following incentives would encourage you to enroll in a car pool program?

CIRCLE ALL THAT APPLY

Reduced fees for car pool parking 1

How long it took to get to work 2

How close to my house it came 3

How frequently it went 4

Extra time off for employees who used it 5

Other 6

SPECIFY: _____

9. What is your job title?

_____

10. What days of the week do you work?

CIRCLE ALL THAT APPLY

Monday 1

Tuesday 2

Wednesday 3

Thursday 4

Friday 5

Saturday 6

Sunday 7

11. What time do you come to work?

_____

RECORD TIME COME TO WORK

12. What time do you leave work?

_____

RECORD TIME LEAVE WORK

13. How many miles do you live from work?

_____

RECORD MILES FROM WORK

14. What city or neighborhood do you live in?

_____

RECORD CITY/NEIGHBORHOOD

	Strongly Agree	Agree	Disagree	Strongly Disagree
15. Having people share transportation is a very good idea.	1	2	3	4
16. The problem of air pollution is overrated.	1	2	3	4
17. Public transportation is a bigger cause of air pollution than cars.	1	2	3	4
18. With the right incentives anyone will support car pooling.	1	2	3	4

19. What is your current marital status? Are you:

Married 1

Divorced 2

Separated 3

Widowed, or 4

Have you never been married? 5

20. Do you have children under 12 living with you?

    Yes 1

    No 2

21. Are you responsible for taking those children somewhere in the morning or picking them up in the evening?

    CIRCLE ALL THAT APPLY

    Yes, taking them in the morning 1

    Yes, picking them up in the evening 2

    No, not responsible for children 3

    No, have no children under 12 4

    Other 5

    SPECIFY: _____

14. The owners of a local health food store want to find out about the lifestyles of community residents, so they design the following questionnaire. What suggestions would you make to the owners?

We have designed the following questionnaire to find out about your healthy lifestyle. It will only take you three minutes to fill out and you will feel much better when you realize how healthy your lifestyle is!

1. Of course you exercise every day, don't you?
   Yes   1   No   2

2. When you exercise do you drink a lot of water? Yes, I drink a lot of water and then I run three miles . . . . . 1 Yes, I drink some water and run four miles. . . . . . 2 Sometimes I drink some water before I run. . . . . . 3 When I run I drink water but when I walk I don't. . . . 4

3. How much do you *avoid* red meat? A lot_____ Some_____ Occasionally_____ When I think of it_____

4. How many people live in your household? Is it just you and one other person, or are there more people there?

        Only me. . . . 1

        Me plus one person 2

        Something else 3

        Who else is there?_____

5. When you finished school, did you have a high school degree and a college degree or something else?

        High school degree and college degree 1

        Something else 2

6. Rank order the following list of things that make for a healthy lifestyle from 1 to 10.

List	Rank
Eating right	_____
Running at least 10 miles a week	_____
Doing meditation	_____
Getting 8 hours of sleep every night	_____
Eating leafy green vegetables every day	_____
Avoiding situations that make you angry	_____
Avoiding caffeine	_____
Never eating sugar	_____
Thinking good thoughts	_____
Lifting weights	_____

15. What kinds of specifications need to be written for the questionnaire in Question 12?

16. What resources would you pursue if you were looking for a source for each of the following types of samples? What are the advantages and disadvantages of each source?

    a. A sample of residences in your local community

    b. A sample of lawyers in your community

    c. A national sample of physicians

    d. A sample of local high school students

17. As the director of nursing services at your local county hospital, you are responsible for a nursing staff of 300. You are contemplating a change in shift hours and want to know how the members of your staff would react to this change. There are 10 service divisions within the department and two shifts on each service, with approximately 15 nurses per service per shift. You have decided that a survey of 100 nurses would be ample to determine what the overall reaction of the nursing staff would be. How would you select a sample, and what means of data collection would you use?

18. a. What are the components of a group self-administered study?

    b. What are the components of a mail survey?

19. You are conducting a mail survey of recipients of Aid to Families with Dependent Children (AFDC) who completed a job training program run by your department last year. You have mailed questionnaires to 300 individuals who have gone through the program and have received only 50 completed returns. You have decided to select another 300 persons to send the ques-

tionnaire to in order to increase the number of responses. Is this appropriate?

20. Make a list of standard sample tracking procedures.

21. You are conducting a mail survey, and you have had several packets returned by the U.S. Postal Service as undeliverable. How would you go about trying to correct each of the following problems?

    a. Address: John Crawford
                   1418 Ork Street
                   Tree Town, OH 76024

      Reason for return: No such street

    b. Address: Mrs. Robert Adams
                   907 River Ave. Apt. #
                   Redbank, NJ 85072

      Reason for return: Undeliverable as addressed

    c. Address: Julius Rosen
                   247 B3 First Ave.
                   New Bedford, MA 456023

      Reason for return: No such number

    d. Address: Doris Newhouse
                   5201 Orange Grove Ave.
                   Orange, CA 91204

      Reason for return: Not in this zip code

ANSWERS

1. Option 4: Individuals in this population should be sufficiently literate that they can respond to a mail questionnaire, and the company should have sufficient money to send out a mail questionnaire. Respondents would also probably be more honest if they complete the questionnaires outside the workplace. Using a questionnaire administered online (Option 5) would be possible if all or most employees have e-mail addresses and the corporation has them on record.

2. Option 3: The PTA wants to solicit the support and participation of active members. Active members are more likely to come to meetings, and they are more likely to be interested in enhancing the school's resources. Passing out questionnaires as members arrive at a meeting increases the likelihood that they will be completed during the meeting and returned at the end. The PTA cannot assume that parents have e-mail addresses unless the organization has previously collected them from active members.

3. Option 6: The fact that the group of interest is elderly and composed of recent immigrants who probably speak Russian rather than English argues against the use of any kind of self-administered questionnaire and for the use of telephone or in-person interviews.

4. Options 1, 2, or 3: The procedures used to test this questionnaire would vary with the amount of resources the clinic has available to develop the questionnaire and the extent to which the clinic staff think that the questionnaire as drafted is incomplete or unclear. One-to-one self-administered questionnaires

would allow the clinic staff to explore patients' responses in the most detail, but this method would make it difficult to administer the questionnaire to large numbers of patients in a short period of time. Group administrations where patients were encouraged to discuss the questionnaire would probably provide more information than semisupervised questionnaires. Both techniques would allow for relatively rapid feedback on the questionnaire. The clinic staff cannot assume that patients have access to the Internet, and it is unlikely that the clinic has e-mail addresses on file for those who do have access.

5. Option 4:   Questionnaires passed out as workers leave the factory would probably provide a fairly representative and rapid assessment of the situation and allow the surveyor an opportunity for answering questions and encouraging returns. Questionnaires administered in groups at work or distributed as workers arrive at work would increase the response rate but also probably increase the likelihood that workers would talk about the questionnaire and that the "squeaky wheels" would have undue influence over the responses. In general, factory workers are not going to respond at high rates to a mail questionnaire, and members of this group cannot be assumed to have access to the Internet.

6. Option 5:   The board has sufficient money and the addresses needed to conduct a mail questionnaire, but not enough money to conduct telephone interviews with 500 people. Although responses will probably be biased toward those with more education, the amount of money available would allow for a substantial amount of follow-up by mail and even by telephone. The responses to a mail questionnaire would be substantially more representative of the county population than would responses to questionnaires

distributed at various community meetings or through the Internet.

7. Option 7:   Two things argue against using any kind of self-administered questionnaire for this study. First, an open-ended question is followed by a closed-ended question that contains a list of problems. If the questionnaire is administered in an interview, respondents will not have that list available when they are asked Question 1, but in a self-administered questionnaire they will. As a result, in a self-administered questionnaire they are likely to select items from the list in Question 2 when responding to Question 1. Second, the list included in Question 2 is long, and respondents are asked to rank order it. This is a difficult task for respondents to do without assistance from an interviewer.

8. Option 6:   This questionnaire has too many open-ended questions and is too complicated to expect students to complete by themselves. It is also subject to misreporting and bias if administered in a school setting, and parents are likely to insist on looking at the questionnaire if it is mailed to students' homes. Researchers have to follow special procedures when participants in *any* kind of research study are under age 18. Generally, these procedures include obtaining permission from each participant who is a minor as well as from his or her parent or guardian. Finally, this is not a very clearly written set of questions, even for a questionnaire used in an interview.

9. a. Yes. The members of the Chamber of Commerce are an identifiable group who should be both motivated to respond and capable of responding to a mail questionnaire. If the Chamber of Commerce has a list of members' e-mail addresses and a substantial propor-

tion of members have access to the Internet, an online survey might be possible.

b. No. The school board might have to undertake some exploratory work to find out how best to conduct this study. Furthermore, up-to-date lists and addresses are unlikely to exist for students who dropped out prior to the current year, and one cannot assume that dropouts would be either motivated to respond or capable of responding to a mail questionnaire.

c. No. Data on childhood immunizations are difficult to get under any circumstances. Individuals must have their records or have parents available who can provide complete listings of the types of immunizations they had as children and the dates of those immunizations. It is unlikely that respondents would be able to provide such information in response to a mail or online questionnaire.

d. Yes. Sorority members can be expected to identify with the organization and be motivated to respond to requests from its leaders. Furthermore, the topic of the study is current and restricted. Recent graduates may have access to the Internet, but because such access currently tends to be inversely related to age, older alumni are less likely to be reachable by e-mail or to use the Internet.

e. No. The manager does not have a list of the names of all persons who regularly patronize the grocery store. The manager would be better advised to interview persons who come into the store over the period of a typical week to find out (a) how they feel about brown eggs, (b) whether they have read the newspaper article, and (c) how regularly they buy groceries at this particular store.

10. a. No. The question is better than the response categories in that it is short and precise, but it contains an assumption that respondents drink the same amount of water every day. In addition, the answer categories are ridiculous. First, many people probably do not know what an ounce represents in volume. It would be better to ask them about "typical cups" or "typical glasses" of water while simultaneously defining the number of ounces in a typical cup (6 ounces) or a typical glass (8 ounces). Second, the range of answers, although mutually exclusive, is not exhaustive; it does not allow for people who drink no water or those who drink more than 14 ounces. Third, the list of responses is unnecessarily long and skewed toward lesser amounts of water. Fourth, because of its length, the list would take up substantial space on a page in a paper-and-pencil questionnaire or on-screen in an online questionnaire.

b. No. This is a burdensome question for a respondent to answer validly without assistance from an interviewer. First, it is open-ended. Second, it asks older respondents in particular to provide a great deal of historical information without giving any guidance as to the *order* in which information should be listed or the *amount* of information respondents should provide about each job.

c. No. The question itself is all right, but the complicated skip pattern set up in the response alternatives argues against its use in a paper-and-pencil self-administered questionnaire. The question might be suitable for use in an online questionnaire, if the program used is sophisticated enough to handle the necessary skips.

d. Yes. This question is short and specific, and the response categories are exhaustive and mutually exclusive. Furthermore, the residual "other" category is unlikely to generate many responses but ensures that respondents who do not feel that the other two answers represent them can express themselves.

e. Yes. This question is short and specific, and the response categories are mutually exclusive and exhaustive if we are interested in finding out about respondents' legal marital status. In some populations, the surveyor might want to add a second question to ask about unmarried cohabitation of either same-sex or different-sex couples.

f. No. This question is even more complex than a double-barreled question. Also, it is open-ended.

g. No. As written, the response categories are not exhaustive; they do not provide for respondents who watch no television or for those who watch equal amounts of television on multiple days. In the question itself, it would be better to say "television" instead of "TV." Although most persons would probably understand the abbreviation, it is always better to be safe than sorry.

h. No. The response categories are fine, and the question is short and precise, but it contains an abstract term (*audited*) and jargon (*IRS*) that not all respondents may understand.

11. The State Department of Parks and Recreation should (a) conduct a literature review to see what, if anything, has been published about leisure time; (b) consider adopting or adapting questions developed by others; and (c) pretest one or more draft questionnaires to

make sure that the final questionnaire is understandable to a representative sample of the state's residents and to estimate the cost of conducting the survey. After pretesting, the department's survey team may decide that it will not be possible to obtain reliable and valid information through a mail questionnaire. The surveyors might also conclude that, because Internet access is only differentially available to residents of the state, it would be difficult to obtain a representative sample using an online survey.

12. No, not as written. The questions are not logically ordered. Within any given topic, the questions are not ordered from less complex to more complex. For example, respondents are asked if they vote before they are asked if they are registered to vote. Respondents are unlikely to understand Question 3 where it is; it should be preceded by Question 7. There are no instructions to the respondent, nor are there any transitions between questions or topics. Question 1, which appears to have been written by a lazy surveyor, is likely to result in many different answers in the residual "other" category that will have to be postcoded.

13. As written, this questionnaire needs four kinds of instructions. First, it needs general instructions, which should appear either in a cover letter or on the first page of the questionnaire. The decision about where the general instructions are to appear should be based on how the questionnaire will be administered. If it is to be distributed at the workplace or as employees arrive for work or leave the workplace, the instructions could appear on the questionnaire itself. If the questionnaire is to be sent to employees' homes, the instructions should appear in a cover letter. The general instructions should explain the purpose of the questionnaire and who is conducting the study, describe how confidentiality will be protected, explain

how respondents were chosen, provide motivation for employees to respond to the questionnaire, anticipate any problems or concerns that employees might have in responding to the questionnaire, provide a way for employees to get more information about the study or confirm its legitimacy, and tell employees how to return the completed questionnaire. If a cover letter is used, it should be printed on letterhead and, if possible, a personal salutation added.

Second, the questionnaire needs brief sets of transitional instructions before Question 1, between Questions 8 and 9, and before Question 19. These instructions should alert respondents to the upcoming topic and to transitions between topics.

Third, the questionnaire needs detailed instructions before Question 15 that explain to the respondent that the following questions are about opinions or attitudes, that there are no right or wrong answers, and how to use the available answer categories. Finally, the questionnaire should close with the following: (a) an open-ended question that encourages the respondent to comment on the questionnaire or add additional information, (b) a thank-you message for the respondent, and (c) a repeat of instructions concerning what the respondent is supposed to do with the completed questionnaire.

14. This questionnaire breaks almost every rule of good questionnaire construction. First, the print is too small. Second, italics are used, which are difficult to read. Third, the owners of the health food store clearly have an "agenda." Their questions do not allow for the possibility that respondents might *not* do the things that the owners consider healthy. Fourth, the response choices for Question 3 are all vague qualifiers. Fifth, there is no consistency in spacing or formatting; some response categories are listed vertically, and others are listed horizontally. Et cetera, et cetera.

15. Questionnaire specifications should document the purpose of the study, how respondents were selected to participate, how the questionnaires were administered, the number and timing of follow-up contacts, and *why* each question or set of questions was included in the questionnaire. If questions were adopted or adapted from other studies, the sources of those questions should be noted, and the reasons for their selection and for any changes should be explained.

16. a. SOURCE: The most ideal source would be a list of 100% of the residences in your sampled community. Short of going out to every street in the area and writing down all of the addresses on each one, you will probably never have such a list; you will probably have to resort to less reliable resources. Check commercial mailing houses, which are the companies that mail flyers, ads, product samples, and the like to households in the area. Contact the local telephone company to determine the rate of unlisted residential telephones in your study area. If the unlisted rate is low, the telephone directory may be an adequate resource. Also, check with the main depot of your local post office, which may be able to recommend a source for addresses.

    ADVANTAGES: Commercial sources usually provide quick, economical access to large numbers of addresses. Often, these resources will be able to provide many of the services required in a survey mailing. They most likely will have computerized lists and therefore will be able to pull a sample according to your sampling specifications, run your address labels for you, fold and stuff your survey materials mechanically, and mechanically post your mailing.

    DISADVANTAGES: The addresses you get when using commercial sources such as mail-order companies and postal addressing firms probably will not include more casual residences, such as garages converted to living space, unless these changes have been made according to local code and the units are legally registered on the local housing rosters as residential addresses. Telephone directories may have high household coverage; however, using them means you will still miss those residences with unlisted numbers. Also, there may be a considerable number of listings in telephone directories with the addresses suppressed. You also cannot tell from telephone directory listings if one telephone covers more than one residence or if one residence has more than one telephone number and therefore has more than one chance of being included in the sample.

b. SOURCE: The commercial listings or Yellow Pages section of your local telephone directory would probably be as good a resource as any. The State Bar Association would be another good source for addresses and possibly e-mail addresses, but it may limit access to its files.

ADVANTAGES: The local telephone directory is an easily available and inexpensive resource. The State Bar Association would most likely have the names and addresses stored on computer, so that accessing and producing a mailing sample would be considerably more time-efficient and possibly more cost-efficient.

DISADVANTAGES: Local telephone directories will miss any lawyers or law groups that have not paid for listings in the commercial pages, so there is the probability that you will miss some individuals in your sample. In the case of law firms, it may be difficult to get the name of each individual lawyer working within a given firm. The State Bar Association may not have current addresses for all individuals.

c. SOURCE: The American Medical Association (AMA) may be able to provide you with a sample of physicians; most practicing physicians are AMA members. If you cannot get a sample from the AMA, you may be able to obtain one from a commercial company that maintains lists of professionals (such as physicians) to sell to interested firms (such as pharmaceutical companies). Many organizations such as the AMA are increasingly including e-mail addresses for members in their membership information files, but the proportion of members covered at this time cannot be assumed to be high enough to be representative of all practicing physicians.

ADVANTAGES: Both the AMA and commercial companies will have computerized files, making it easy to select a sample and produce mailing labels.

DISADVANTAGES: Getting in touch with an appropriate and cooperative individual in the AMA may require extra effort. Neither resource is free, and neither will have 100% coverage, but the AMA will probably have a more complete listing of practicing physicians. Neither list may be 100% up-to-date on current addresses. It may be especially difficult to get the names of individual physicians who work in group practices or who work for health maintenance organizations.

d. SOURCE: Contact the administrative offices of your local school district for public schools and individual administrative offices for private schools. You will have to obtain permission "systemwide" to be able to access any information. Once you have obtained this access, you will have to contact the high schools you have selected for inclusion in your sample. Different schools may place different conditions on how you access students. If you are not taking a 100% sample in the classroom, you may have to use identification numbers for sampling rather than names because you may not be given access to individual names. You may be asked to distribute a letter requesting signed permission from a parent or guardian of each student to have him or her participate in your study. This will probably have to be coordinated through the student's homeroom teacher. If and when you have obtained parental consent, you will probably also have to obtain consent from each student. If you are not allowed access to students' home addresses, you may have to arrange for group administration of your survey at some time when all students are in one place, such as homeroom or assembly, or supply each student with a packet to be completed at some later time and either mailed back or returned to a designated location at the school.

If you are denied access by the school board, you may have to resort to using a convenience sample— that is, you might go to places in your community where high school students are accessible, such as church groups, fast-food outlets, and other such attractions. You may find a situation where you can conduct a group administration or at least hand out forms to be completed at another time and returned by mail.

ADVANTAGES: A school-based sample of students essentially guarantees that nearly every student in your area has the possibility of being selected. The group setting allows for group administration or distribution, maximizing the number of individuals you can survey in one contact. Although you may need to spend considerable time in obtaining access, there is virtually no cost in obtaining the sample.

Convenience samples are generally easy to access. The costs to obtain such samples are minimal, and the data can be collected in a very short period of time.

DISADVANTAGES: School-based samples are fine if all you want to represent are students. If you are interested in representing teenagers, you will miss that portion of the population that has dropped out of school. If you use a school-based sample, any student who is not present at school on the day of your administration or distribution will not have an opportunity to participate in the study. Therefore, your sample will have less chance of being truly representative.

Convenience samples can be extremely biased and may be limited in their representativeness. For example, if you go to video arcades, you will find only those students who go to these types of amusements. The return rates on this type of sample may also be extremely low, because there is little incentive for potential respondents to participate unless the topic is of overwhelming interest.

17. Each service/shift should be sampled for 5 respondents; $15 \div 5 = 3$. Make an alphabetical list by service and by shift of all nurses on the staff. Take every third name. To avoid possible influence from coworkers and to protect respondent anonymity, you should mail the questionnaires to the nurses at their home addresses and provide stamped, self-addressed envelopes for the return. You cannot assume that the nurses have access to the Internet.

18. a. Group Administration Packet Checklist

✓ Sample
    Access? Means of selection

✓ Schedule
    Calendar of date/time/place

✓ Informed consent
    If necessary. Quantity?

✓ Cover letter
    Print quantity?

✓ Questionnaire
    Print quantity?

✓ Incentive (if used)
    Quantity?

✓ Other handouts (if any)
    Quantity?

✓ Means of retrieval
    Collect/box/mail back?

b. Mailing Packet Checklist

✓ Sample labels/addresses
    Quantity?

✓ Outgoing mail envelopes
    Sample size?

✓ Size of questionnaire?
    Additional materials?

✓ Outgoing postage
    Metered or stamped?

✓ Cover letter
    Print quantity?

✓ Questionnaire
    Print quantity?

    ✓ Incentive (if used)
        Quantity?

    ✓ Other inserts (if any)
        Quantity?

    ✓ Return mail envelope
        Postage-paid business
        reply/metered/stamps?

19. No. If you do not use a follow-up to increase response rates from the original sample or track bad addresses, you may be missing important feedback about the success of your program. For example, the program may have been highly successful; a significant number of individuals may have obtained good jobs and moved on, and so are no longer at their original addresses. Conversely, the program may have had very little impact on most of the respondents' lives, and they are not motivated to respond. If you use replacement sampling, you will probably never receive responses from either of these types of participants, and you will not have accurate information with which to evaluate your program.

20. SAMPLE TRACKING PROCEDURES GUIDELINES

   - Check for typographical and/or clerical errors in addresses.

   - Stamp outgoing envelopes "RETURN SERVICE REQUESTED" and correct the address file based on corrected returns.

   - Check with the sample provider for address updates (if applicable).

   - Check telephone directories, telephone directory information, and reverse directories.

   - Check with local utility companies and/or the state's department of motor vehicles.

   - Remail packets to all corrected addresses.

21. a. Check with your sample source; if the address is the same in the source's files, in this case there is probably a typographical error in the street name. "Ork" is a fairly unusual name for a street. Look for a likely name spelled similarly, such as "Oak." If an Oak Street *does* exist in the sampled area, try readdressing the packet to that address.

b. Check with your sample source for the missing apartment number. If the source's listing is the same, try to determine the correct apartment number by checking the appropriate telephone directory. If the name is listed with a telephone number, you can try calling the number, explaining your purpose, and asking for the correct address. If the building is accessible to you, you might look at mailboxes or the building directory to see if you can determine the correct apartment number. If you cannot find the number, try leaving "Apt. #" out of the address entirely; if the postal carrier knows the name, he or she might deliver the packet even without the apartment number on the address.

c. In this case, the apartment number appears to have been put before the street name, so that is appears to be a part of the street address. Readdress the packet with "B3" following "First Ave." The unit number should always appear after the street name or on the next line.

d. The wrong zip code was used in this address. Zip code directories are available at the main branches of many public libraries, or you can call the U.S. Postal Service's toll-free information line (800-ASK-USPS) to get the proper zip code for the address. In this case, the final number of the zip code was one digit off; it should have read 91203. You should be aware that in some areas, zip codes can differ within a single block.

Suggested Readings

Aday, L. A. (1997). *Designing and conducting health surveys* (2nd ed.). San Francisco: Jossey-Bass.

Basic textbook on the design and administration of all kinds of surveys. Draws on methodological work on surveys in general and health surveys in particular.

American Association for Public Opinion Research. (1997, May). *Best practices for survey and public opinion research and survey practices AAPOR condemns.* Ann Arbor, MI: Author.

Overview of issues surveyors should consider in designing questionnaires and surveys; assembled by one of the major professional organizations in the area of survey research.

American Association for Public Opinion Research. (2000). *Standard definitions: Final dispositions of case codes and outcome rates for surveys: RDD telephone surveys, in-person household surveys, and mail surveys of specifically named persons.* Ann Arbor, MI: Author.

Describes how surveyors should calculate and report response rates for surveys administered by in-person interview, telephone interview, and mail questionnaire.

Aquilino, W. S. (1994). Interview mode effects in surveys of drug and alcohol use. *Public Opinion Quarterly, 58,* 210-240.

Reports the results of a field experiment designed to study respondents' willingness to admit use of illicit drugs and alcohol in three conditions: personal interviews that incorporated the use of a self-administered questionnaire to

*obtain the sensitive information, personal interviews without a self-adminis-
tered questionnaire, and telephone interviews. The use of a self-administered
questionnaire within a personal interview resulted in somewhat higher estimates of illicit substance use, and telephone interviews resulted in somewhat
lower estimates.*

Beebe, T. J., Harrison, P. A., McRae, J. A., Anderson, R. E., & Fulkerson, J. A.
(1998). An evaluation of computer-assisted self-interviews in a school setting. *Public Opinion Quarterly, 62,* 623-632.

*Reports on a study in which students were randomized between self-admin-
istered paper-and-pencil questionnaires and computer-assisted self-inter-
viewing. Response rates for sensitive questions were found to be consistently
higher for the paper-and-pencil administration.*

Berry, S. H., & Kanouse, D. E. (1987). Physician response to a mailed survey:
An experiment in timing of payment. *Public Opinion Quarterly, 51,* 102-114.

*Compares the response rates of questionnaires mailed to physicians when
$20 was included in the original mailing with those promising $20 upon
receipt of the completed questionnaire. Prepayment was found to have significant positive effects on response rates.*

Bourque, L. B., & Clark, V. A. (1992). *Processing data: The survey example.*
Newbury Park, CA: Sage.

*Provides a systematic explanation of how to perform data processing using
today's technology. The authors adopt a broad definition of data processing
that starts with selecting a data collection strategy and ends when data
transformations are complete. Much of the material covered has direct applicability to the design, administration, and processing of self-administered
questionnaires.*

Bourque, L. B., Cosand, B. B., Drews, C., Waring, G. O., Lynn, M. J., Cartwright,
C., & PERK Study Group. (1986). Reported satisfaction, fluctuation of
vision, and glare among patients one year after surgery in the Prospective
Evaluation of Radial Keratotomy (PERK) Study. *Archives of Ophthalmology,
104,* 356-363.

*Provides a description of the PERK Study population and how results of the
surgery related to satisfaction and side effects 1 year after surgery on the
first eye.*

Bourque, L. B., Lynn, M. J., Waring, G. O., Cartwright, C., & PERK Study
Group (1994). Spectacle and contact lens wearing six years after radial
keratotomy in the Prospective Evaluation of Radial Keratotomy Study.
Ophthalmology, 101, 421-431.

Describes the PERK Study population 6 years after surgery on the first eye and 5 years after surgery on the second eye. The questionnaire used in this study is the basis for the questionnaire discussed in the examples in this book.

Bradburn, N. M. (1983). Response effects. In P. H. Rossi, J. D. Wright, & A. B. Anderson (Eds.), *Handbook of survey research* (pp. 289-328). New York: Academic Press.

Focuses primarily on questionnaires used in interviews. However, information presented on open versus closed questions, question order, question length and wording, and retrospective memory have relevance for the design of all questionnaires—including self-administered ones.

Brook, R. H., Ware, J. E., Rogers, W. H., Keeler, E. B., Davies, A. R., Donald, C. A., et al. (1983). Does free care improve adults' health? Results from a randomized controlled trial. *New England Journal of Medicine, 309,* 1426-1434.

One of the first major publications that reported the results of RAND's Health Insurance Experiment. Includes a description of the design of the study and the data collection techniques used.

Church, A. H. (1993). Estimating the effect of incentives on mail survey response rates: A meta-analysis. *Public Opinion Quarterly, 57,* 62-79.

Reports the results of a meta-analysis of 38 experimental and quasi-experimental studies that implemented some form of incentive so as to increase response rates in a mail survey. The use of prepaid monetary or nonmonetary rewards included with the initial mailing was compared with the use of monetary or nonmonetary rewards provided conditional upon return of the questionnaire. The effects of incentives were found to be modest, with those that included rewards in the initial mailing being more effective in increasing response rates.

Converse, J. M., & Presser, S. (1986). *Survey questions: Handcrafting the standardized questionnaire.* Beverly Hills, CA: Sage.

Succinct overview of what is involved in designing questionnaires, with particular attention to questionnaires administered in interviews and studies that focus on attitudes and opinions. Much of the information provided has relevance, however, to self-administered questionnaires.

Council of Professional Associations on Federal Statistics. (1993). *Providing incentives to survey respondents: Final report.* Washington, DC: General Services Administration, Regulatory Information Service Center.

Addresses the gathering of statistical data and matters of confidentiality.

Couper, M. P. (2000). Web surveys: A review of issues and approaches. *Public Opinion Quarterly, 64,* 464-494.

One of the best overviews of online surveys available to date.

Couper, M. P., Traugott, M. W., & Lamias, M. J. (2001). Web survey design. *Public Opinion Quarterly, 65,* 230-253.

Reports findings from three experiments that examined how design characteristics influenced whether students at the University of Michigan completed online surveys and the answers they gave.

Dillman, D. A. (1978). *Mail and telephone surveys: The total design method.* New York: John Wiley.

Classic reference on the design of mail questionnaires. A "must" for those interested in developing expertise in this area.

Dillman, D. A., Singer, E., Clark, J. R., & Treat, A. B. (1996). Effects of benefits appeals, mandatory appeals and variations in statements of confidentiality on completion rates for census questionnaires. *Public Opinion Quarterly, 60,* 376-389.

Reports on a study that examined the effects in a national sample of 30,000 of two different prominently displayed appeals in combination with two different prominently displayed confidentiality assurances on mail-back completion rates for census questionnaires. Only the mandatory appeal significantly improved completion rates.

Dillman, D. A., West, K. K., & Clark, J. R. (1994). Influence of an invitation to answer by telephone on response to census questionnaires. *Public Opinion Quarterly, 58,* 557-568.

Reports on an experiment on a national probability sample that compared completion rates for a census questionnaire when respondents were given the option of calling a toll-free number to respond rather than mailing the questionnaire back. Availability of the telephone option increased response rates only when it was included in a follow-up letter that did not include a replacement questionnaire.

Fink, A., & Kosecoff, J. (1998). *How to conduct surveys: A step-by-step guide* (2nd ed.). Thousand Oaks, CA: Sage.

"How-to" book good for both novice and more experienced surveyors. Presents realistic purposes, goals, and examples.

Fowler, F. J., Jr. (1993). *Survey research methods* (2nd ed.). Newbury Park, CA: Sage.

Comprehensive summary of the methods of survey research and the sources of error inherent in each. Provides a guide for calculating survey statistics and error measurement.

Fox, R. J., Crask, M. R., & Kim, J. (1988). Mail survey response rate: A meta-analysis of selected techniques for inducing response. *Public Opinion Quarterly, 52,* 467-491.

Reports the results of a meta-analysis of the experimental studies that have examined 10 different factors felt to influence response rates to mail surveys. Results indicate that such things as advance letters, sponsorship, color of paper, type of postage used, and follow-ups increase response rates. Increases in the amount of a monetary incentive appear to result in decreasing marginal gains in response rates.

Gubrium, J. F., & Holstein, J. A. (Eds.). (2002). *Handbook of interview research: Context and method.* Thousand Oaks, CA: Sage.

Good encyclopedic reference on interviewing across all data collection methods. Includes a good overview of Internet interviewing.

Henry, G. T. (1990). *Practical sampling.* Newbury Park, CA: Sage.

Sampling textbook designed for the "common surveyor." Not overly technical, but highly practical.

James, M. J., & Bolstein, R. (1990). The effect of monetary incentives and follow-up mailings on the response rate and response quality in mail surveys. *Public Opinion Quarterly, 54,* 346-361.

Reports on a study that compared the separate and joint effects of monetary incentives and follow-up mailings on response rates. Four mailings without an incentive produced a higher response rate than a single mailing with an incentive, but a combination of follow-up mailings and a higher monetary incentive produced higher response rates than follow-up mailings without an incentive. There was, however, some evidence of response bias across the different treatment groups.

Jobe, J. B., & Loftus, E. F. (Eds.). (1991). Cognition and survey measurement [Special issue]. *Applied Cognitive Psychology, 5*(3).

Special journal issue representing a collaboration intended to blend, or merge, the scientific value embedded in laboratory settings with that found in naturalistic research settings, and to do so under conditions that make possible the emergence of a methodologically innovative, mutually support-ive interdiscipline.

Kaldenberg, D. O., Koenig, H. F., & Becker, B. W. (1994). Mail survey response rate patterns in a population of the elderly: Does response deteriorate with age? *Public Opinion Quarterly, 58,* 68-76.

Reports on a study in which four-page questionnaires were mailed to a prob-ability sample of 1,000 retired public employees. On average, the response rate declined by 0.5% for each unit of age examined. The effect of age on quality of response is unclear.

Kalton, G. (1983). *Introduction to survey sampling.* Beverly Hills, CA: Sage.

Good primer on sampling theory for the beginning surveyor. Provides useful illustrations, emphasizes practical considerations, and discusses problems surveyors are likely to encounter in sampling.

Kraemer, H. C., & Thiemann, S. (1987). *How many subjects? Statistical power analysis in research.* Newbury Park, CA: Sage.

Introduces a simple technique of statistical power analysis that surveyors can use to compute approximate sample sizes and power for a wide variety of research designs.

Kraus, J. F. (1990). Homicide while at work: Persons, industries, and occupa-tions at high risk. *American Journal of Public Health, 77,* 1285-1312.

One of the articles examined in the literature review conducted in prepara-tion for the Workplace Assault Study. A study of work-related homicides in California from 1979 to 1981 found an average annual rate of 1.5 homicides per 100,000 workers with a male:female ratio of 4.2:1. Rates were highest for police (20.8), security guards (16.5), and taxi drivers (19.0) and were ele-vated for persons who worked at night in retail or service jobs, such as con-venience store clerks, bartenders, and janitors.

Kruger, R. A. (1994). *Focus groups: A practical guide for applied research* (2nd ed.). Thousand Oaks, CA: Sage.

Provides a detailed discussion of the focus group technique. Describes char-acteristics, conditions of use, and implementation.

Krysan, M., Schuman, H., Scott, L. J., & Beatty, P. (1994). Response rates and response content in mail versus face-to-face surveys. *Public Opinion Quarterly, 58,* 381-399.

Compares response rates for an hour-long in-person interview with those for a shorter mail questionnaire. Both surveys were administered in Detroit in 1992. Response rates did not differ between the two methods for white respondents but were significantly lower for black respondents who received mail questionnaires. Responses also differed by administrative procedure, with respondents to the mail questionnaire expressing more negative attitudes toward racial integration and affirmative action.

Rasinski, K. A., Mingay, D., & Bradburn, N. M. (1994). Do respondents really "mark all that apply" on self-administered questions? *Public Opinion Quarterly, 58,* 400-408.

Reports on a study in which questions with instructions to "mark all that apply" were compared with questions where each of the applicable categories was asked in a "yes-no" format. Respondents who were presented with the "mark all that apply" format selected fewer response options than those presented with the "yes-no" format, but it is not possible to tell from this data set whether this means that "mark all that apply" formats result in underreporting or "yes-no" formats result in overreporting.

Riopelle, D. D., Bourque, L. B., Robbins, M., Shoaf, K. I., & Kraus, J. F. (2000). Prevalence of assault and perception of risk of assault in urban public service employment settings. *International Journal of Occupational and Environmental Health, 6,* 9-17.

Reports findings from the Workplace Assault Study, which is used as an example throughout this book.

Schaefer, D. R., & Dillman, D. A. (1998). Development of a standard e-mail methodology: Results of an experiment. *Public Opinion Quarterly, 62,* 378-397.

Examines how various combinations of mail and e-mail information and reminders influenced the response rates of Washington State University faculty to an e-mail survey.

Schuman, H., & Presser, S. (1981). *Questions and answers in attitude surveys: Experiments on question form, wording, and context.* New York: Academic Press.

Reports the findings from a series of experiments conducted to determine the influence of the ways in which questions about attitudes are asked on the data obtained.

Schwarz, N., & Hippler, H.-J. (1995). Subsequent questions may influence answers to preceding questions in mail surveys. *Public Opinion Quarterly, 59,* 93-97.

Reports on a study that compared the effects of question order on responses in telephone surveys and mail surveys. In telephone surveys, responses to the index question were influenced only if the contextual questions preceded the index question, whereas in mail surveys, responses to the index question were influenced if the contextual questions either preceded or succeeded the index question.

Sheatsley, P. B. (1983). Questionnaire construction and item writing. In P. H. Rossi, J. D. Wright, & A. B. Anderson (Eds.), *Handbook of survey research* (pp. 289-328). San Diego, CA: Academic Press.

Basic reference on how to develop questions and questionnaires. Includes information on issues that researchers should consider in deciding whether questionnaires are an appropriate method for collecting data and on the use of various kinds of administrative procedures.

Sudman, S., & Bradburn, N. M. (1982). *Asking questions.* San Francisco: Jossey-Bass.

Describes the development of questions used in structured questionnaires, or interview schedules, used in social and market research. Covers general issues in questionnaire design; the development of questions on nonthreatening and threatening behaviors, attitudes, and demographic characteristics; the development of response categories; and question wording and context.

Tanur, J. (Ed.). (1992). *Questions about questions: Inquiries into the cognitive bases of surveys.* New York: Russell Sage Foundation.

Provides a thorough airing of questions about the rigid standardization imposed on the survey interview. Contributors show how traditional survey formats violate the usual norms of conversational behavior and potentially endanger the validity of the data collected.

U.S. Bureau of the Census. (1992). *Census of population and housing: 1990, United States. Summary Tape File B* [Computer file]. Washington, DC: U.S. Department of Commerce (producer); Ann Arbor, MI: Interuniversity Consortium for Political and Social Research (distributor).

Source of 1990 Census data reported in Chapter 2.

U.S. Bureau of the Census. (2001). QT-02. Profile of Selected Social Characteristics: 2000. Data set: Census 2000 supplementary survey summary tables. Geographic areas: United States and California. Retrieved October 5, 2001, from http://factfinder.census.gov/servlet/qttable?_ts=20628101640

Source of 2000 Census data reported in Chapter 2.

U.S. Department of Health, Education, and Welfare, Overseer of State Programs. (1994). *California WIC Program manual* (Publication No. WIC 210-60). Washington, DC: Author.

Source of the information reported in Chapter 2 on the federal Women, Infants and Children Program, which is administered at the state level.

Ware, J. E., Jr., Snow, K. K., Dosinski, M., & Gandek, B. (1993). *SF-36 Health Survey: Manual and interpretation guide.* Boston: New England Medical Center, Health Institute.

Describes some of the scales developed out of RAND's Health Insurance Experiment and Medical Outcomes Study. Provides information about questions included in the PERK Study.

Warriner, K., Goyder, J., Gjersen, H., Hohner, P., & McSpurren, K. (1996). Charities, no; lotteries, no; cash, yes: Main effects and interactions in a Canadian incentives experiment. *Public Opinion Quarterly, 60,* 542-562.

Reports on an experiment that examined whether response rates to mail surveys differ when prepayments of cash, charitable donations, or chances to win a lottery are used as incentives. Response rates were highest and earliest when a cash incentive was included with the questionnaire.

Washington State Department of Labor and Industries. (1993). *Study of assaults on state employees at eastern and western state hospitals.* Tacoma: Safety and Health Assessment and Research for Prevention.

One of the studies examined in the literature review for the Workplace Assault Study. In a study of two Washington State psychiatric hospitals, questionnaire responses were compared with injuries reported in various official reports. The numbers of assaults reported were roughly comparable for incident reports and questionnaire responses. However, Workers' Compensation and OSHA logs substantially underestimated the total number of occurrences in a given period. Whereas 12.4 injuries per 100 nursing FTEs (full-time equivalents) were reported in OSHA logs, 21.6 to 28.7 workers' compensation claims were made, 63.4 to 70.9 assaults per 100 FTEs were reported in incident reports, and more than 70% of the ward staff completing questionnaires reported experiencing at least one physical assault leading to mild injury.

Weisberg, H. F., Krosnick, J. A., & Bowen, B. D. (1989). *An introduction to survey research and data analysis* (2nd ed.). Glenview, IL: HarperCollins.

Relatively sophisticated presentation of survey research methods, with greater focus than most guides on data analysis, report writing, and the evaluation of completed surveys.

Wentland, E. J., & Smith, K. W. (1993). *Survey responses: An evaluation of their validity.* San Diego, CA: Academic Press.

Reports on a meta-analysis (of 37 studies conducted between 1944 and 1988) that assessed the accuracy of individuals' responses to questionnaires when compared with independent criteria. Discrepancies varied with the extent to which the requested information was accessible to respondents, subject matter, and characteristics of the questionnaire.

Yammarino, F. J., Skinner, S. J., & Childers, T. L. (1991). Understanding mail survey response behavior: A meta-analysis. *Public Opinion Quarterly, 55,* 613-639.

Reports on a meta-analysis of studies that investigated how various aspects of mail survey design affect response rates. Results indicated that repeated contacts in the form of preliminary notification and follow-ups, appeals, inclusion of a return envelope, postage, and monetary incentives effectively increased response rates.

Glossary

Abstract term—A term that is complex and thus difficult for some people to understand. Sometimes surveyors cannot avoid using abstract terms in questionnaires, but whenever possible they should consider providing synonyms or definitions of the terms for respondents.

Adaptation of questions—The survey researcher's practice of using established sets of questions but changing them to make them more appropriate for the current study. Examples include translating questionnaires and using questions that were originally designed for self-administered questionnaires in a survey administered by interview. Researchers should be cautious in adapting questions. They must always give full credit to the persons who originally designed the questions and, when possible, consult with the designers when making decisions about adaptation.

Administration of questionnaires—The process by which questionnaires are distributed to and filled out by respondents. Questionnaires may be administered by interviewers as part of in-person or telephone surveys, or they may be filled out by respondents either in group settings (such as classrooms or workplaces) or as individuals.

237

Adoption of questions—The survey researcher's practice of using sets of questions that were developed by other researchers exactly as they were developed. When surveyors adopt questions, they must give full credit to the person or group who developed the questions.

Advance letter—A letter sent to a potential study participant that explains what the study is about, who is conducting the study, and how the data will be protected and used; indicates who will be contacting the potential respondent and when that contact will take place; and provides information about how the recipient of the letter can obtain further information.

Anonymous data—Data that, once collected, can never be connected to the person or organization that provided the information.

Answer categories (or response categories, or response choices)—The set of responses to a closed-ended question from which a respondent selects his or her answer(s).

Bias—The tendency for researchers to project their own perceptions, behaviors, and knowledge onto the participants in their studies. The presence of bias can affect a study in such a way that it does not obtain a complete picture of what is happening in a population. Researchers can reduce bias by using appropriate methods in designing and conducting their studies.

Branching—A technique for varying the number of questions and the sequence in which questions are asked in the survey instrument through the use of skip patterns. Branching allows the surveyor to tailor the questionnaire so that it can gather data from different respondents with different experiences.

Closed-ended question—A question for which the respondent is provided with a series of alternative answers to choose among.

Coding—The assignment of numbers to verbal data for purposes of entering the data into computer programs for analysis.

Computer-assisted telephone interviewing (CATI)—Survey interviewing conducted over the telephone in which the questionnaire is programmed into a computer along with information about the sample. The interviewer reads the questions to the respondent from a computer monitor and records the respondent's answers directly into the computer.

Confidentiality—Protection of a respondent's identity. To ensure confidentiality, survey researchers make sure that individual respondents cannot be identified within a data set, usually by stripping all identifiers (e.g., telephone numbers) out of the data file and reporting findings only in statistical groupings.

Control—The survey researcher's power to manage both who participates in the study and the order in which data are collected.

Cover letter—A letter that accompanies a mailed questionnaire that explains what the study is about, who is conducting the study, and how the collected information will be used.

Data collection—The process of gathering information about individuals, groups, agencies, households, organizations, and so on. Data can be collected using questionnaires, through observations, or from records.

Demographic data—Data that describe the characteristics of a person, household, or organization; demographics include information about age, gender, education, income, and racial and ethnic identity.

Double-barreled question—A single question that actually asks two questions rather than one.

Estimate of time (for questionnaire completion)—Approximation of the amount of time an average respondent should take to complete the questionnaire. One purpose for conducting pretests and pilot studies is to estimate how long respondents will take to complete questionnaires, so that modifications can be made if necessary. A potential respondent should be provided with a realistic estimate of the time it should take to complete the questionnaire.

Exhaustive response list—A list of alternative answers provided for a closed-ended question that includes answers that comfortably and appropriately represent all persons studied.

Exploratory study—A study in which the researcher is assessing whether a particular topic is worthy of research and whether research can feasibly be conducted on the topic.

Follow-up mailings—A mailing in which reminders are sent to potential respondents to encourage them to complete an interview or fill out a questionnaire and return it.

Font—A size and style of typeface used in a written document.

Formatting—The process of setting up a data collection instrument so that it can be easily understood by interviewers and respondents. Elements that surveyors need to consider in formatting include the use of space and consistency in the style of questions, instructions, and answer alternatives.

General instructions—Instructions for the respondent that introduce the study and explain what it is about, who is sponsoring it, and how the data will be used. General instructions may be presented in a cover letter or at the beginning of the questionnaire.

Grid—A question format used for sequences of questions that have similar objectives. By using grids in questionnaires, surveyors can save space and link related data appropriately.

Group administration—The filling out of a self-administered questionnaire in a group setting. Each person completes the questionnaire without consulting other persons in the group, but the surveyor or another supervisory person is available to provide introductory instructions, answer questions, and monitor the extent to which questionnaires are completed as well as how much individual respondents communicate with each other during the period of administration.

Illiteracy—The inability to read and write. In the United States, it is estimated that 20% of the adult population is unable to read and write in English.

Implementation—The multistage process of preparing and administering a survey and processing the questionnaires.

Incentives—Money, services, or goods provided to respondents in order to encourage their participation in a study.

In-person (or face-to-face) interviewing—Interviewing in which the interviewer and the respondent are in the same place, often the respondent's home, and can see each other.

Interviewer—A person who is hired and trained to interview respondents for a study.

Jargon—Specialized language that is usually associated with a particular professional group or work group. Acronyms are a form of jargon. Like slang, jargon should not be included in questionnaires.

Language barrier—An obstacle to a potential respondent's participation in a study owing to the fact that he or she

GLOSSARY

does not speak and/or read one of the languages in which the study is being conducted.

Letterhead—Stationery with a preprinted heading, address, and other information that identifies an organization. Printing correspondence with potential respondents on letterhead helps establish the legitimacy of a study and may increase some individuals' motivation to participate.

Literacy—The ability to read and write.

Literature search—The survey researcher's examination of published books and articles for reports on theories and prior studies concerning the researcher's topic of interest. Conducting a literature search is one of the first steps in developing a survey design and a questionnaire.

Logical ordering of questions—The organization of the questionnaire so that related questions are together and not mixed in with or interrupted by other topics.

Machine-readable—Readable by a computer. Data need to be set up in machine-readable form so that they can be entered into a computer for analysis.

Mail questionnaire—A self-administered questionnaire that is mailed to a potential respondent.

Mailing—The coordinated sending of a questionnaire or advance letter through the mail such that all those individuals to whom the material is sent receive it at approximately the same time.

Motivation—The desire to participate in a study. The topic of a study often influences a person's motivation to participate, and the methods used in the design of a study also affect motivation. In an interview survey, the interviewers themselves can affect motivation.

Mutually exclusive response list—A list of alternative answers to a closed-ended question in which all choices are clearly independent of one another, so that the respondent has no trouble selecting the response that best describes him or her.

Objectivity—Neutrality, or the careful avoidance of bias, in the way the researcher designs and administers the study.

Online survey—A survey in which the questionnaires are administered via the Internet. This kind of survey is of increasing interest to researchers.

Open-ended question—A question on a questionnaire that includes no preset list of possible answers for respondents to choose among.

Order effects—The influence that one set of questions (or answer categories) may have on the answers respondents provide to later sets of questions.

Paper-and-pencil administration—Administration of a questionnaire in which the data collected are recorded on a paper copy of a questionnaire or on a related answer sheet.

Pilot study (or pilot test)—A full testing of all aspects of the study, including the selection of subjects and the full collection of all data. A pilot study is a "study in miniature."

Population—All of the individuals, households, institutions, or organizations that meet a certain criterion (e.g., live in California).

Precoding—The assignment of variable names to each question and numeric codes to each answer alternative before the questionnaire is actually administered, so that data can be entered into a computer efficiently as interviews are completed.

Pretesting—The process of testing parts of the questionnaire during questionnaire development, generally with a convenience sample of respondents who are thought to be the "most different" on the section of the questionnaire being tested (e.g., a researcher would pretest on both males and females, both older persons and younger persons, or the like). (Note that this is the primary meaning of the term *pretesting* as it is used in survey research; it should not be confused with the same term often used to mean the data collection that takes place before the administration of an intervention in an experiment or quasi-experiment.)

Primacy effect—The tendency of respondents, when answering closed-ended questions, to select the first answer heard or read rather than considering the full list of alternatives.

Probability sample—A sample for which the researcher can estimate how likely it is that each person, household, or other unit in the population will get into the sample.

Progress indicator—A graphic element used in some online questionnaires to indicate to respondents how much of the questionnaire they have completed and how much remains to be completed.

Question-answering instructions—Instructions for respondents in the survey instrument that specify how they should go about answering particular questions.

Questionnaire—An instrument containing a structured, standardized sequence of questions that is used in an interview or filled out by a participant in a study.

Questionnaire specifications—Complete documentation by the researcher of the purpose of the study, how the sample for the study was selected, how the questionnaire was administered, where and why questions were included in the questionnaire, and how individual questions were handled.

Recency effect—The tendency of respondents, when answering closed-ended questions, to remember and select the answer they heard or read last rather than any of the prior alternatives.

Reliability—The reproducibility of the survey data. That is, data are considered to be reliable when the same distribution of characteristics, experiences, behaviors, or attitudes would be obtained in data collected at a different time, by a different data collector, or using a different methodology.

Residual "other" category—An unspecified option included in the answer categories provided in response to a closed-ended question. Including such a category is particularly valuable when the researcher is not sure that the list of alternatives provided is exhaustive.

Response rate—The proportion of people, households, or institutions that are selected for a study from whom or about which data are successfully collected.

Sample—The individuals, households, institutions, or organizations selected out of a population for study. There are three primary types of samples: probability, systematic, and nonprobability.

Sample frame—A list of individuals, households, institutions, organizations, or phone numbers that represents the population and from which the sample is selected.

Self-administered questionnaire—A questionnaire that is filled out personally by the respondent.

Semisupervised administration—The filling out of a self-administered questionnaire in a setting where the level of supervision is very low. Instructions given to respondents may vary in such settings because respondents receive instructions individually and possibly from different people.

Sensitive topic—A topic that respondents may be reluctant to discuss with researchers. Sexual behaviors and illegal behaviors are among the topics generally thought to be sensitive.

Simple random sampling—A type of probability sampling in which the researcher uses a random numbers table or random numbers generator in a computer to select persons from the population or sample frame. In this form of sampling, the fact that a particular person is selected for the sample does not influence who the next person selected will be.

Skip instructions—Instructions within a question in a questionnaire that allow branching to occur and so enable data collection to be modified for respondents with different characteristics, experiences, knowledge, and attitudes.

Slang—Words and phrases developed within and used by particular groups. Slang sets the members of one group off from those of other groups and functions as a shorthand form of communication. Because not all respondents are likely to understand slang terms, surveyors should not include them in questionnaires.

Sponsorship—Financial and other support provided by organizations or other groups for the conduct of a study.

Standard question battery—An existing set of questions that has been widely used in prior research studies.

Stratified sampling—A type of probability sampling in which the population or sample frame is first divided into sections, or strata, and then simple random sampling procedures are used to select the sample within each section.

Subjectivity—A form of bias in which the researcher perceives that respondents are "like" him or her, or that he or she "knows" what respondents think and do. Subjectivity is the opposite of objectivity.

Survey—A system for collecting data from a population or sample at one point in time where it is assumed that there is heterogeneity in personal characteristics, attitudes, knowledge, and behaviors across the population.

Telephone interviewing—A data collection method in which interviewers administer the survey instrument to respondents by telephone.

Tracking—The monitoring of data collection, including the extent to which the sample is being used up or exhausted. Appropriate tracking may show the need for more follow-up mailings, the need to draw another sample replicate, and so on. The term *tracking* is also sometimes used in reference to trying to find correct contact information for particular respondents or potential respondents.

Transition—A point within a questionnaire where questions on one topic end and a new topic is introduced. Transitions are usually marked by transitional statements or instructions.

Transitional instructions—Instructions for respondents that appear in the questionnaire where questions on one topic end and questions on another topic begin. Transitional instructions give respondents a chance to "catch their breath" and help them change the focus of their thinking.

Translation—The process of converting a questionnaire that was written in one language into another language. Generally, two translators are used: The first translator translates the questionnaire into the second language, and the second translator performs a back-translation—that is, translates the first translated version back into the original language.

Unsupervised administration—The filling out of a questionnaire by the respondent with no help or supervision from anyone else.

Vague qualifier—A modifying term that may be interpreted differently by different people. Most adverbs can be considered vague qualifiers.

Validity—The degree to which the data being collected really represent the range of experiences, opinions, behaviors, and types of people present in the population being studied.

Vertical format—A questionnaire format in which the alternative answers to closed-ended questions appear under each other rather than listed horizontally. The advantage of this format is that interviewers, respondents, and data entry personnel can see and differentiate among the various alternatives easily.

About the Authors

Linda B. Bourque, Ph.D., is Associate Director of the Center for Public Health and Disasters, Associate Director of the Southern California Injury Prevention Research Center, and Professor in the Department of Community Health Sciences in the School of Public Health at the University of California, Los Angeles, where she teaches courses in research design and survey methodology. She has conducted research on ophthalmic clinical trials, intentional and unintentional injury, and community perceptions of and responses to disasters. She is author or coauthor of 60 scientific articles and the books *Defining Rape* and *Processing Data: The Survey Example* (with Virginia Clark).

Eve P. Fielder, Dr.P.H., has more than 35 years' experience in survey research. Since her early work in market research, she has been involved in all phases of survey design and administration and has conducted hundreds of surveys, both commercial and academic. For the past 30 years, she has been with the Institute for Social Science Research at the University of California, Los Angeles, where she is Director of the Survey Research Center. She has also taught survey research methods at UCLA and at the University of Southern California. She has consulted on studies for numerous organizations and community service agencies and has a strong background in cross-cultural research.